Pat,
"Eye" se[e]s book #2 ...
"Doubles" your pleasure
s/[?]

9/27/14

I'm The One The Other Isn't - Book Two
MORE
Stevie - Stanley Stories

By
Stanley E. Toompas, O.D.
Stephen E. Toompas, R.Ph.

Stanley E. Toompas

Headline Books, Inc
Terra Alta, WV

I'm The One The Other Isn't - Book Two
MORE Stevie - Stanley Stories

copyright ©2013 Stanley E. Toompas, O.D., Stephen E. Toompas, R.Ph.

All rights reserved. No part of this publication may be reproduced or transmitted in any other form or for any means, electronic or mechanical, including photocopy, recording or any information storage system, without written permission from Headline Books, Inc.

To order additional copies of this book, for book publishing information, or to contact the authors:

Headline Books, Inc.
P. O. Box 52
Terra Alta, WV 26764
www.HeadlineBooks.com

Tel/Fax: 800-570-5951
Email: mybook@HeadlineBooks.com
www.headlinebooks.com

ISBN-13: 978-0-938467-54-0

Library of Congress Control Number: 2012948211

Toompas, Stanley E., Toompas, Stephen E.
   I'm the one the other isn't - book two more Stevie-Stanley stories by Stanley E. Toompas, O.D. and Stephen E. Toompas, R.Ph.

ISBN-13: 978-0-938467-20-5
1. Memoir 2. Philippi WV.
Non-Fiction

PRINTED IN THE UNITED STATES OF AMERICA

"We know it sounds funny,
But we're not in it for the money,
We don't need a reputation,
And we're not in it for the show!"

(Paraphrase of The Raspberries/Eric Carmen
1974 hit song "Overnight Sensation")

Foreword and Dedication

We dedicate this second collection of Stevie - Stanley stories, the ones NOT used as bedtime stories for our children, to our children. Collectively speaking, though their Father and Uncle are hyper individuals, borderline OCD, undiagnosed ADD, definitely IBS, historically ulcerated, and possessing many idiosyncrasies, all four children are normal/typical young Americans (A credit to their respective Mother's influence, of course.)

During the publishing process, Stephen's eldest daughter, Amanda, turned 27 years old. She is an elementary school teacher. His youngest child, Shelby, age 20, attends college at West Virginia University. Stanley's son, Christopher, also age 20, attends college at West Virginia Wesleyan. Stan's daughter Kelsey, 18 years old, is a 2012 high school graduate and now attends Fairmont State University.

It is our sincere hope, in spite of the fact that WE are their fathers, that somehow, years from now, our children will view their own childhoods as favorably as we have ours. We twins were loved and cherished, and so are they.

Background and History

We are Stanley and Stephen Toompas. We introduced ourselves to you last year, when we published our first book, *I'm The One The Other Isn't, The Stevie - Stanley Stories*. We are identical twins, born on April Fool's Day, 1958, in Clarksburg, West Virginia. Sheltered and over-protected as youth, nonetheless the unique circumstances of our childhood created wonderful memories.

Our first book captured those memories in a collection of thirty-one short stories. Childhood tales we had related to our own children as bedtime stories. It took over thirteen years for the initial idea of writing our stories to come to fruition as a published book. We hope all of our family, friends, acquaintances, and patients/customers enjoyed our collection of childhood memories as much as we did writing them. We thank our publisher, Cathy Teets of Headline Books, for making a dream come true.

In fact, we enjoyed writing the first book so much, that we decided to write this sequel. This second book contains twenty-two other Stevie-Stanley Stories that we did NOT share as bedtime stories with our children. These are longer "short" stories (Is that an oxymoron by chance?) and the majority are from the teenage years and beyond. A couple of the stories were difficult to share and proved that even our wonderful life was not perfect.

Through the years, in Stephen's Drug Store, or Stanley's Optometric office, after being overwhelmed by our loquacious nature and silly sense of humor, a customer/patient might exclaim, "You sure are one of a kind!" Either of us, respectfully, would momentarily pause to absorb the compliment, but then just as swiftly "come clean." We revealed the truth to our customer or patient by saying, "Well, thanks, but I'm really not one of a kind. I have an identical twin brother." Surprised (stunned is more accurate) by this revelation, people can't believe it. We then say, "Having an identical twin does prove one thing in life ………. God sure has a sense of humor!"

We spent our entire adult life developing our individuality and our separateness, so to speak. It is humbling to realize that neither our first book, nor its sequel would be interesting or engaging or even publish-worthy if it weren't for the collective; the fact that WE are skinny, small, slow, and uncoordinated identical twins, born on April Fool's Day, raised in a "metal" house, etc.

So, as people routinely ask an identical twin when he is alone, "Are you, you? Or are you, your brother?" Our answer remains consistent; "I'm the One the Other Isn't."

We hope you enjoy book #2 of the Stevie-Stanley stories.

I'm The One The Other Isn't - Book Two
MORE Stevie - Stanley Stories

Foreword and Dedication 5
Background and History 6

The Stories:
1) Gin's Pick-Up 9
2) Double, But No Trouble 15
3) The Twin's Towers 23
4) Putter in Our Hands 27
5) Survival 31
6) Slim Twins 37
7) Sex 43
8) Cleaning Shelves 49
9) Chess Kings 53
10) The President's President 57
11) Twins, Taught a Lesson 65
12) Cruising The Burger Chef 73
13) EGGed On 77
14) Second Chance in the Second City 83
15) The "Non-Campaign," Campaign 89
16) Double Dose 93
17) Double Vision 96
18) Double Trouble 101
19) Silver Celebration 105
20) Separation Day 110
21) Let's Talk (We're Good At It) 114
22) Twin Beds 124

Gin's Pick-up

As grade school students, Stevie and Stanley's small, intimate world seemed magical. It was a low risk and logical extension of our sheltered home life. In the mid-1960's, our school days began with a good-bye kiss from Mom at the door of the "Metal House" (The metal house we grew up in was called a Lustron home. It was manufactured of multiple 2-foot square wall panels of enamelcoated steel and erected upon a concrete slab. All living space was on one level, there was no basement and no second floor. The homes were developed after the close of World War II by the former Lustron Corporation. About 2,500 of these curious homes were built before the company collapsed, and we twins lived in a light tan-colored one, on 115 Mandan Road in the Nixon Plaza area of Clarksburg adjacent to Nutter Fort, West Virginia. Think of it as a house constructed of an Erector Set, but on a much greater scale.), a walk along our driveway, and then we may have "skipped" out Mandan Road together. Meeting up with other kids along the way, we would turn onto Cimarron Road as we continued the short distance toward school.

At the end of Cimarron Road, where the neighborhood street intersected with the main road, Buckhannon Pike, we could see the grade school positioned on top of the hill. Sometimes, as we approached this point, we looked up and saw nothing but a white cloud. Pausing to discuss the situation, as we gazed toward the fog enshrouded Nutter Fort Elementary school, we twins hypothesized that the school was gone. It had certainly disappeared over night. Other more enlightened children bet us that it was still there. So, we began walking toward the school again to discover who was correct. We really wanted to be right, and hoped to approach the top of the hill and encounter nothing but baron soil. Every time, however, the school "magically" reappeared the closer our proximity to it. We still argued with our friends that it had really been gone, but that God had replaced it with an identical one. And who better to know about things "identical" besides us?

Our memories tell us that, except for third grade, most days in grade school went well, and then after a typical enjoyable day at school, we headed home. However, we did not always retrace our steps on our return trip. A large percentage of the time, prior to entering Cimarron Road, we turned onto Maryland Avenue and walked one block toward the conveniently located neighborhood store on the corner of an alley. Naturally, this was before society labeled such establishments as "convenience stores." This small store had limited physical space yet seemed to have everything. It was the epicenter of our known universe and was called, Gin's Pick-up.

The owner was Virginia Stewart, but all the kids called her Gin. Stevie and Stanley did not actually know her last name until we became adults. She eventually became a customer of Stephen's at Town and Country Drug Store and an Optometric patient of Stanley's. Stephen actually lived next door to Gin for a couple of years in the mid 1980's! She seemed to like us.

Gin's Pick-up was a grade school student's dreamland even though it had a concrete floor, and the corners of the store were very dim in the winter months. This lighting problem was remedied in the summer months when Gin kept a side door as well as the front door opened constantly. The store was stocked with candy bars, candy cigarettes, pixie sticks, suckers, gum of an infinite variety including mini-Chicklets and Bazooka bubble gum, Pez along with Pez dispensers, taffy, lifesavers (with their flavor-specific, identity-indicating display case), jaw breakers, fire balls, carbonated beverages, notebooks, binders and colorful folders, a variety of pencils, mechanical pencils, pens, erasers, squirt guns, 45' records, comic books including the "Fantastic Four," and our favorite, "Mad" or "Cracked" magazines. She had a freezer full of ice cream bars, popsicles, Nutty Buddies, ice cream sandwiches, fudgesicles, orange sherbet filled Push-ups, frozen candy bars such as Reese cups, and our favorite, plastic cups of frozen ice cream. If purchased, Gin would give you a small individually wrapped, paper-sealed, flat wooden paddle type spoon to eat with. We twins thought this was really neat-o!

The store stocked corn chips, potato chips, nuts, pretzels, popcorn, cheese crackers, peanut butter and cheese crackers, Twinkies, Hostess cupcakes, and pepperoni rolls that we assume are indigenous to West Virginia (Note: They are awesome. But, if you travel West across the Ohio river, or North past the Mason-Dixon Line, or venture East of the Appalachians, you soon discover that seemingly all people that you encounter from out-of-state, are ignorant of this traditional West Virginia staple.) Gin's would always have the latest fad available for the grade school kids to buy, whether it be mood rings, rat fink rings, trolls, cap guns, packs of ball cards or monster cards with gum, or packs of goofy stickers. We used these stickers to decorate our colorful paper folders, or our book covers that we had either purchased or made from brown paper grocery bags. Of course, Gin's had milk, bread, newspapers, and many other "grown-up" items associated with today's convenience stores, but we paid no mind to that.

If Mom had given us a couple of dimes, or even a quarter to share, we anxiously anticipated our trip to Gin's. Of course, we realize that if you are not of our "baby boomer" generation (born between 1946 and 1964), you are probably wondering what in the world could the twins purchase for a quarter? Well, we twins are pretty sure that every item that we listed was in our price range! For example, if we twins both purchased a frozen Reese cup, and gave Gin a quarter, we got a dime back. By the early 70's tax became an issue and if you gave her a quarter for a 25-cent item, she would ask where your pennies were. Quickly realizing that we twins had none, she would wave us out of the store.

We distinctly remember riding our bikes (without helmets) from our home to Gin's on the 4th of July to buy fireworks. We purchased smoke bombs, "snakes," little fire crackers, poppers, and our favorite, sparklers. We do not recall if Gin provided us with matches or not. We never hurt ourselves with these items. If we had, it would have been due to our own carelessness, not her responsibility nor society's fault.

If we became hot while riding our bikes on a mid-summer day, or thirsty after shooting basketball on the unshaded Ohio Avenue courts, Tom Fogg's back driveway, or in Richard White's front driveway, we did not go home for water, and there was no bottled water back then. Instead, we rode to Gin's Pick-up, purchased a bottle of refreshing Coke, popped the cap off with the bottle-cap opener attached to the side of the cooler, and paid Gin. We then either sat on the wall out front of the store and drank it, or just as often, mounted our stingray bicycles, grasping the handle bars with our left hand and the glass bottle of Coke in our right, and rode away.

In our first book, we reported being awkward and clumsy as kids, and for the most part we were. But this particular action required a lot of coordination! Remember, this was not a "forgiving" plastic resealable bottle of pop! Once it was open...it was open. If we had dropped it, we would not only have spilled the pop, but most certainly would have shattered the glass bottle. We never recall having dropped one! Our only explanation for this is that we actually became quite accomplished bicycle riders. We uncoordinated Toompas twins became almost "normal" upon mounting our stingrays; analogous to Gomer Pyle becoming melodic Jim Nabors with a microphone. We must admit, however, that no matter how adept we were at simultaneously drinking "pop" and peddling, that childhood buddies

Eddie Bee and Mike Swain were much better at "popping" or "riding" wheelies.

The only parking at Gin's Pick-up was along the street. Since it was located in a residential area, it got crowded at times. So, by today's standards, it would not have been very convenient. Nonetheless, it remained a consistently busy store. It closed many years ago and was torn down. Ironically, the property was purchased by Stanley's hometown bank from Barbour County, and a "convenient" branch banking facility was built.

We Toompas twins miss this store. If we both close our eyes and concentrate, we can see ourselves depositing our blue and white, banana seated, Roadmaster Stingray bicycles onto the narrow patch of grass alongside the store. As we run through the front door, we twins are wearing identical outfits right down to our Keds sneakers. Unable to distinguish us, one from the other, Gin is watching us intently from behind the counter, adjacent to her enormous cash register. We can actually feel the cold air of the freezer in front of the counter hit our faces as we reach in for a delicious treat. It is a very hot day, so after painstakingly making our selections we tarry further and hold the lid open so that just a little more soothing cold air engulfs us. We skinny twins are instantly cooled to our marrow. Gin urges us to shut the lid immediately. We obey and as we hand over our coins to Gin, she smiles. Everything is once again alright in the world. Stevie and Stanley have no bills to pay, no emergencies, no worries or stress. We are at the epicenter of our childhood universe once again at...*Gin's Pick-up*.

I'm The One The Other Isn't-Book Two

Double, But No Trouble

Stevie and Stanley began each day of grade school with the reciting of the Pledge of Allegiance, a quick check to see if our hands and fingernails were clean, and whether we possessed a handkerchief or not. A clean, safe, and ideal learning environment, we twins have clear and pleasant memories of our experiences at Nutter Fort Elementary School. Our teachers, Mrs. Snider, Mrs. Crigler (who lived two doors down the street from us), Mrs. Fulmer, Ms. Kulczycki, and Ms. Gimble were all outstanding and we admired them. There was one exception however, Ms. Grake, the third grade teacher! We believe she had a paddle fetish. She carried a paddle with her at all times. She tapped the paddle against her off hand readying for an opportunity or excuse to use it, which now, looking back, seemed to excite her! She found a reason to use her paddle almost every day. In fact, she punished us identical twins if we ever fooled her by trading places, whereas other teachers found it humorous. Once, Ms. Grake lifted Stevie and placed him in the trash can! Excluding third grade and its daily paddle threat, learning seemed effortless in this comfortable and controlled environment. So seamless was the educational process that we thought school was really fun.

There were two classrooms for each grade respectfully at Nutter Fort Elementary School. Though, just across the hall, as far as grade school memories are concerned, the other classroom might as well have been across the ocean! For example, Stephen's wife Kim (Johnson) lived just out the street from us, but was in the other classroom, so only a first grade play and after school walks home are shared experiences.

You must remember, as explained in our first book, that we had no "color" at our metal home. But, the bedroom tile being the only exception, neither was it "black and white." Our world was definitely a shade of gray! The steel walls and ceilings of our home were made of drab gray metal panels. No pictures or family photos hung from our walls, anywhere in our house. Ever! Why? There were no magnets appropriate or powerful enough for support. Our "loud" red carpet in the living room was actually a welcomed reprieve from our monochromatic home interior.

In comparison, our elementary school classroom seemed a kaleidoscope of color. It was bright, well lit, inviting, clean, and comfortable. A joyful and enjoyable environment. With pictures, photos, vivid teaching tools, and posters, our intimate surroundings were visually pleasing every day of the school year. Grade school was not only exciting but perceptually soothing for us. We both can easily visualize each classroom but we cannot specifically describe textbooks that we used at school. The only vivid recollections were of thick workbooks and a multitude of 8 x 11 mimeographed worksheets and their unique aroma. Combining this smell with the intoxicating scent of the white paste we used, it's no wonder we enjoyed school so much!

We do remember the shape and feel of our desks and the pocket-filled storage cloth coverings for the back of the seat. It was always an exciting time when Mr. Tanner, the janitor, came to adjust "up" the desk's writing surface, making all aware that you had grown!

Of course, we tiny twins never ever remember experiencing "that" proud moment!

The smartest, highest achieving classmate in grade school, without a doubt, or peer, for that matter, was Pam Baker. Pam was the best at everything: reading, writing, spelling, math, science, music, and art! Stephen recalls that she was the first student to have a "64" count crayon box, with a built in sharpener on back! Most kids only had 8-12 count packs, or if fortunate, 24. He envied her and lobbied at home for his own "big" box. Eventually he did receive a "48" count box. Not quite Pam's, but larger than most others.

More important to us however, was not who was the smartest, but who was best at eraser tag! We assume that everyone reading this is well aware of this universally known classroom game. The unquestionable, unflappable, undisputed, undefeated, understood champ every year throughout grade school was our friend Steve Metzgar. The top of his head seemed to be flat. We believe that once an eraser was set there, it never moved, no matter how much he did. He was always the champ, unless he was sidelined by a nosebleed which he repeatedly suffered. Only then would someone else temporarily reign as class champion. We twins were decent, but not so accomplished. Yes, we had very narrow, so-called "flat" faces, but the top of our heads seemed shaped like an egg. A difficult perch on which to balance an eraser.

Speaking of erasers, we always enjoyed being chosen to "dust" the erasers.

This, as you may recall, is the process where two students were selected to go outside to "bang" the erasers together and rid them of the majority of chalk dust. We twins viewed "dusting" the erasers as an award for good behavior or grades. We do not recall ever being paired together for this task however. Inhaling dense clouds of chalk dust was apparently of no immediate medical concern nor did we suffer any long-term health-related consequences.

Stevie and Stanley both had speech problems, and that makes sense since we were identical twins. Back then, placing the word "sense" and the word "since" together in a sentence would have been a nightmare for us! We were "special" as we were trotted off with a couple of other students for speech lessons. We must have had undiagnosed hearing problems also. For example, we twins used the word "hickycaboose" when describing the last car of a long train. We must have been confused when our grandmother had said the phrase, "Hitch the caboose." Our word, "bombernade" was another one. It was a combination of "bomb" and "grenade." We have no idea how that became part of our vocabulary.

During grade school we took tap dance lessons with Mr. Louie. He would begin the lessons with the record…Shuffle step…Shuffle step…Right foot…Left foot. Repeat, repeat, repeat! We did not learn to dance, or tap, nor did it help with our coordination, but the record is indelibly engrained in our memory. Shuffle step, Shuffle step… somewhat analogous to how your soul is permeated with the song *Its a Small World After All* after visiting Disney World. Years later, as an adult, Stephen took some dance lessons concurrently with his daughters and actually performed a number on stage. Mr. Louie sure would have been proud.

Even with all the positive experiences, Sixth grade was the first time we recall a teacher telling us directly that we were smart, and that, yes, we could do it, whatever "it" was. This teacher was Ms. Kulczycki. There were a few classmates that were "bragged on" throughout grade school because of their smarts, and rightly so. We had not been included among those…till now. She altered our outlook by making us look inward. A new self- awareness began evolving. From that point on both of us were always near the top of our class academically. We believed we were smart because she believed we were. Ms. Kulczycki was a great teacher and one of our favorites. We respected her. So much so, that in later years, we would sneak by her room, pause, and clear our throat so she would notice us. The kids in her class would giggle at the sight of identical twins, and then she would take a moment to greet us and proudly introduce us to her class. Of course, like everyone else, she had no idea which one of us was Stephen and which one was Stanley. But that was okay, because she really did think WE were special after all.

It was also in sixth grade that we began understanding that we were raised differently. We realized we were over-protected compared to other boys. Three examples come to mind. First, our parents made us wear galoshes over our shoes! We got by with this early on in grade school, but as the years passed, we were teased endlessly about our "rubbers." We soon quit using them. Secondly, our jackets had hoods and Mom demanded that we use them. It seemed that no other boy had a hood on their jacket, and if they did, they certainly did not utilize it. Bigger boys would grab us by our hoods, and since we were so lightweight, pull us around by it! Today's popular "hoodies" were just NOT cool in 1969! Ditto earmuffs.

The final example is even more embarrassing than the other two, if that is at all possible. In the Spring of 6th grade, other boys were riding their bicycles to school and we begged our parents to let us also. They did not agree at first but after multiple requests, they finally compromised. They decided that it would be okay, if, and this is a big "IF," we mounted baskets on our bicycles!

Of course, if you are an adult reading this, you understand this practical and pragmatic apparatus. School books could be placed in the basket so to free your hands while riding home. Well, no other boy, and we mean none, had baskets but us. Our blue stingray Roadmaster bikes became a subject of ridicule and we were laughed at incessantly. We removed the baskets as soon as summer break began.

It must have been 1970 when Sam Huff the former great linebacker for West Virginia University in the 50s and the New York Giants in the 60s, stopped by our classroom for a brief moment. Upon seeing him at the door, without permission, Stanley immediately left his seat and went straight to the door to greet him. Stanley told Mr. Huff that our Dad had taught us that he was the greatest football player ever. Sam smiled, asked his assistant for one of his football photos, and signed it as he explained his current candidacy for the US House of Representatives. He then handed it to Stanley and opined that our Dad must be a smart man. Stanley still has this Sam Huff autographed photo in his procession some 40+ years later. (Note: Sam lost the election to Bob Mollohan.)

Throughout our time in grade school, one day each year stood out; April 1st.

Not only was it our birthday, but it was April Fool's Day. It seemed that all of our classmates always made an extra effort to plan a way to play an April Fool's joke on the twins. We remember arriving at school, happy in the knowledge that it was our birthday, but forgetting about the fooling part. Unprepared, we were both fooled multiple times by our aware and alert classmates. The students were really creative concerning this and seemed to derive great pleasure in fooling the birthday boys. Truth be known, we twins enjoyed the attention.

Halloween was a favorite time for both of us also. The school parties during the day, and the "trick or treat" at night were fun, but the best part was the fact that for this one day, we twins were allowed to be different from each other! Sporting unique costumes, we looked nothing alike. For a short while, we had our own identities. One a lion, the other a skeleton. (Appropriate don't you think, considering just how "boney" we were.)

We seemed insulated from the "Real" world at Nutter Fort Elementary. Even though the Viet Nam war was raging at the time, we were mostly unaware. We do recall seeing a map of Viet Nam projected on our black and white TV by the evening news, and seeing numbers that represented death tolls, but by and large, we were oblivious. In about the 5th grade, we remember watching Walter Cronkite discussing the war on TV, and praying that we would never have to go to that strange place far away. Sad as it may be, truth be known, we have more vivid memories of Jack the TV repairman replacing vacuum tubes during a "house call," or laughing hysterically at the TV while watching Herman's hilarious adventures in "The Munsters" than we do of "Uncle" Walter. Also, we were completely unaware of Lyndon Johnson's "Great Society" initiatives. Was the President unaware of OUR great society that was already in place right here in Nutter Fort, West Virginia?

Most of our grade school classmates went on to attend junior high and high school with us. However, there was some attrition along the way. We twins look back fondly at our class composite photographs. But we wonder, what ever happened to Sonja Wilson? Kathy Leasburg? Karen Dennison? or for that matter, Freddie Ball? The vast majority of our classmates turned out fine, and it probably had a lot to do with our wonderful school and dedicated teachers.

    An annual ritual in early January was to stop briefly at Wilson's furniture store located right below the grade school. We would enter and sheepishly request a calendar for the New Year. The gracious employee would hand us a small box. Opening the box upon arriving home, we would find two pieces, the plastic base, and a plastic insert embossed with the current year supporting 12 individual slips of paper representing the 12 months. For some reason, these just thrilled us! Too many years have passed to explain why, and so many years have passed since we attended Nutter Fort Elementary School, but suffice it to say that, during our grade school years, Stevie and Stanley were...*Double, But No Trouble*.

I'm The One The Other Isn't-Book Two

The Twin's Towers

As we have repeatedly reminded the readers, we twins were skinny, small, slow, uncoordinated, and lacked common sense. We can be forgiven for our deficit in common sense considering the unique circumstances in which we were raised: Living in a metal house, hiding in a closet or running away from thunder and lightning storms, and living with ONLY an absolute, indistinguishable, interchangeable, almost exact identical twin. Further more, if this weren't enough, we were born with no talents. Absolutely none! Unless, of course, you consider "talking" a talent. In that case, as adults, we would both be highly decorated award winners. Sadly to say, no such accolades exist.

Even though we had no talents, our immediate family loved and cherished us, and of course, we always had each other. Still, to eventually be successful in life, we required more. All young children, we twins being no exception, needed adults of good character as role models in their lives. Stevie and Stanley were fortunate to have been surrounded by such people.

We had relatives with high standards that served as wonderful role models, with the prime examples being Uncle Bud and Aunt Dot Stanley. Along with Grandma Irene, they lived nearby and directly influenced us for the entirety of our childhood. Uncle Bud, a pharmacist, was our Mom's brother, but was more like a brother to Dad. Compassionate, fair, an ardent WVU sports fan, and always optimistic, Uncle Bud coached the church league basketball team that we played on. Aunt Dot was always well-read, thoughtful, and sincere. Their four children, our cousins Mark, Leslie, Bruce, and Jeff, are the embodiment of their essence. We feel uniquely blessed to be related to them.

"Big" Walt and Dottie-Jean Cleavenger also positively influenced our childhood. Parents of our cousins, Beth and Walt, who we introduced to you in our first book, both were patient and unselfish adults. They moved to Virginia when we were in third grade. Forty-five years have passed since then, yet Dottie-Jean has never failed to send us a birthday card each April Fool's Day!

Also, from an early age, Dad and Mom surrounded us with their exceptional contemporaries and friends. Respected individuals that we emulated.

These role models or "towers" were as follows:

1) Jim and Connie Caravasos: Jim a Pharmacist, and Connie a nurse, moved away to Morgantown when we were seven years old. We have some vivid and pleasurable memories. Jim loved VW Bugs and flew model airplanes. Both were fun-loving and possessed friendly dispositions.

2) Raymond and Rose Goodwin: Rose was Mom's best friend, a dedicated and devoted lifelong friend. Many times, Rose was the calm during the storms for Mom. Raymond was a tranquil, exceedingly patient individual, possessing a quiescent temperament. Little Rae's parents both loved to sing in the church choir.

3) Edgar and Marguerite Moore: Mr. Moore was a Pharmacist at Bland's when Dad began practicing. Organized, knowledgeable and mannerly, he was passionate about his multiple aquariums full of unique fish and his coin collection. Mrs. Moore was reserved and polite.

4) Hubert and Nell Smith: Our neighbors across the street from the metal house on Mandan Road. We called him "Smitty." He was a very hard-working and principled man. He watched out for us. He walked everywhere, as he and Nell did not own a car. Nell, was sweet, kind, friendly, and an excellent baker. They were the Grandparents of our childhood friend, Lisa Boomer. They were just like Grandparents to us.

5) Rosanne and Paul Huey: We called her "Nini." We have no idea why! With no children of their own, they certainly enjoyed spending time with us. We can still remember the "Mr. Magoo" toys they bought for us!

6) Marvin and Helen Layfield: Friends of Dad's in high school, Marvin was also a college roommate at WVU. Marvin was a confident and loyal man who lived and worked in Houston. Helen was always good-natured, friendly, and dedicated to her family. We loved Marvin's 1949 Chevy.

7) Ron and Roberta Smith: Ron was a brother to Terry Smith, a Pharmacist who was a business partner of Dad and later Stephen. Terry offered great advice to Stanley during his confused college days. Ron and Roberta lived in an apartment near our junior high school. Ron would encourage us to stop by after school to play games such as Rock'em - Sock'em Robots, table hockey, or electric football. Affectionately known as a "big kid," Ron also owned an awesome 350, 4-speed, 4-barrel, 1970 Chevy Nova SS, green with a black vinyl top. We enjoyed the rides home more than the toys! Ron was friendly and fun. Roberta is as sincere and consistent in 2012 as she was in 1972.

8) Don and Carolyn Hutson: A Pharmacist, Don was Dad's business partner for about 35 years. Don reports, for purpose of this text, that he and Dad only had one significant disagreement in all those years! He can not recall the specifics. As recorded in our first book, Stevie and Stanley referred to him respectfully as, "Uncle" Don, due to the close relationship. Everyone that knows Don would concur that he is a man of integrity, high morals, and high standards. Possessing unquestionable character, Don is compassionate, caring

and concerned. He has been a significant part of our lives and simply put, we love him like an Uncle! "Aunt" Carolyn is a beautiful person and always nice. Paired with the handsome Don, as young adults, they may have served as the inspiration for "Ken & Barbie." Truth be known, cousin Leslie had her first "crush" on "Uncle" Don, and Stanley had his first "crush" on "Aunt" Carolyn.

Just for completeness sake, we need to inform you that Don knew Stanley well. He advised Stanley and discussed with our Dad on his behalf, that Stanley probably should enter into public relations, acting, or politics, not health care. Though optometry has worked out well for Stanley, he admits, that at times he has fantasized about acting, envisioned being a United States Senator, and fancied himself an eventual author. Well, check one of the list.

All of our parent's friends were good people and served as excellent role models. They were all quintessential good American Citizens. Trustworthy, honest, dedicated, committed, accountable, goal-oriented, honorable, and loyal, they possessed these and numerous other virtues that made an ever-lasting impression on us.

Stevie and Stanley were skinny, small, slow, uncoordinated, possessed little common sense, and were endowed with no obvious talents. However, we twins were blessed abundantly with good role models who served without coercion as...*The Twin's Towers*.

Putter in Our Hands

We mentioned our fondness for mini-golf in our first book. Let us state, for sake of completeness, that if our family was ever traveling around the state for vacation, and saw a miniature golf course, we begged our Father to stop and play. It usually took only a minimal amount of pleading on our behalf, as Dad thoroughly enjoyed it also. For some reason, we recall that Mom never played. Never! This is verified by the multiple scorecards found in Stanley's scrapbook.

When we were Kindergarten age or so, we do recall playing a mini-golf course that existed in Bridgeport on Route 50. The only specific memory was of the last hole. It was extremely elevated. As is customary for mini-golf establishments, a hole-in-one on this last hole won the golfer a free game. We twins were not concerned about that however. We just thought it was really neat how the ball disappeared down a long tube and into the clubhouse when hit into the hole! The course was closed in the mid 1960's.

The Clarksburg/Bridgeport area did without mini-golf until about 1970, when a course was built at Norwood Park in Nutter Fort.

Stanley and Stephen loved the bright colorful golf balls, and the creative and imaginative layouts of each hole. We played often. During the summer of 1971, it seems as though we played every day, multiple times per day. Sometimes, we would complete a game, ride our metallic green, 3-speed stingray Schwinn bikes home, get a quick drink, get some more money, and ride back to the park to play another round. While other kids were at the pool swimming, or playing baseball on the adjacent fields, we twins found a place where we were not ridiculed or constantly embarrassed by our skinny physiques and lack of coordination.

We played the Norwood Park course so often, that we figured out how to make a hole-in-one on the majority of holes. So, we were confident when tournament time arrived and believed we would win the "club" championship. We truly envisioned that together we could beat any other pair of mini-golfers....We were wrong! In the very first round, playing against the team of Steve Winters and Bruce Jenkins, we choked. One of us would miss a putt, then the other, then we began blaming one another for our misfortune. Stanley and Stephen were very disappointed. We just yearned to be the best at something, and we thought mini-golf was THAT something!

We loved mini-golf so much, that we pleaded for Dad to help us construct a couple of makeshift "holes" in our back yard. Failing to convince him of this great outdoor idea, we turned our attention inside. You may recall our Dad's putting machine that we mentioned in the chapter "Our Toy Story" from our first book. We would place this putting machine in various locations in our metal house. We would then start at the most distant point and compete. It was like putting on an ice rink when putting from the tile floors of the bedrooms or kitchen. Mom's throw rugs mimicked "the rough." The carpeted concrete slab of the living and dining area also served as a "fast" putting service. Mom just hated it when we hit the ball with excessive force. The ball would contact the metal walls and a loud tinny sound would echo throughout the house as the ball would ricochet then bounce across the carpet. We had a blast! Today, kids would need complex video games to stay occupied.

By the way, if you are a tall but un-athletic individual who is tired of being asked the following by short people; "Do you play basketball?" We have some advice for you. When a person approaches, looks up at you, and poses that question, look down and calmly reply, "No! Do you play mini-golf?"

As teenagers, we sometimes would take our girlfriends on a date to Norwood Park and play mini-golf. As young adults, we would vacation at Myrtle Beach. The Kims liked soaking up the sun at the beach. We twins, on the other hand, enjoyed the numerous thematic miniature golf courses.

Even now, 50+ years old, it is hard to pass up a miniature-golf course. Just find us a course, pay the fee, and off we would go with...*Putter in Our Hands*.

I'm The One The Other Isn't-Book Two

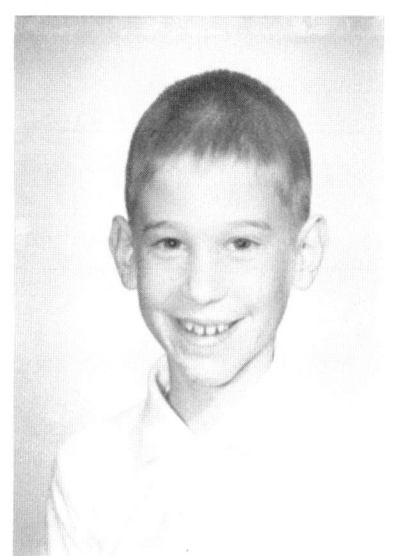 

Survival

As we have told you, grade school in the 1960's was fun. Nutter Fort Elementary School in Nutter Fort, West Virginia, was a fairly new facility and full of fantastic teachers and classmates. From the teachers, to Mr. Tanner, the janitor, to the cooks in the cafeteria, all adults were "looking out" for the students, including Stevie and Stanley.

Usher in the 70's and everything changed. We began junior high school in 7th grade, in the basement of Roosevelt-Wilson High School in Nutter Fort, West Virginia. It was a half century old, less inviting facility, in stark contrast to the modern elementary school. Gone were the modern "green" chalk boards, ancient pitted "black" boards were now the norm. For the most part, the teachers such as Mr. Kulczycki (brother to the aforementioned 6th grade teacher) and Mrs. Compton were so good, that they made you forget the shortcomings of the surrounding structure. In fact, their instruction in Science and Math, respectfully, was so thoroughly competent, that we both credit them for guiding us down the path which eventually led us to become healthcare professionals.

However, that's the good news. The rest of this story is not so pleasurable. In fact, so uncomfortable were we with these memories, that we suppressed them and did not inform our parents about what we are about to reveal, until long after we had completed college!

Physical education class was a mandatory requirement in junior high school. It took place in the gym across the back alley from the main building. The dressing room was in the basement, adjacent to the varsity basketball locker room. Heading down the very narrow, brick lined staircase seemed similar to descending into a dungeon on an Alfred Hitchcock horror movie. The dressing room was a damp, musty, malodorous, inadequately lit and cramped facility. There was a constant drip, drip, drip of leaking plumbing continuously emanating from the communal showers. The benches had splinters, the brick lined walls were hard and unforgiving, and the cement floor, slick. All of these hazards could be overcome under normal circumstances. However, the gym teacher was not as observant nor as mindful as those of our other classes, and herein lay the problem.

Upon changing clothes either before gym class or afterward, the crowded, rarely supervised changing facility was full of peril for we skinny, undeveloped, late-blooming Toompas twins. Weighing in at under 70 lbs., we were the smallest kids in the class and the object of humiliation and bullying. Our physical appearance would have reminded most people of 3rd graders instead of 7th! We were so small and skinny at age 12, that when our parents took us to an establishment that allowed all children under 6 to enter free, they frequently offered this deal to our Dad!

We quickly learned that the less time spent in the changing area, the better. So, we minimized our "before gym" time in the dressing room by wearing our required gym trunks and t-shirts, under our school clothes. Sure, we had to sit through first period class with an extra layer of clothes on, but this was quite preferable to actually changing in the dangerous dressing room. So, this routine reduced the time spent in the dressing room before gym, which was advantageous, but did nothing to alleviate our problems afterward.

The boys we knew, that had attended grade school with us, were fine. The real problems were the flunkies, older boys who were repeating 7th grade. They made our life miserable. We twins were the subjects of their brutality and cruelty. We were both hit, pushed, physically hurt, shoved, poked, pulled, pinched, battered, and bruised. Sometimes bleeding was the result. (And we thought dodge ball was brutal during class!) It is amazing that the physicality did not result in a broken arm or leg, considering just how thin we were! There were times that these bullies pulled our arms behind our backs, so far beyond the apparent normal range of motion, that we thought they would snap like a turkey "wishbone!" We can distinctly remember those thought processes. We even had knives pulled on us. Of course, we could not inform the gym teacher or our parents because these bullies warned us that if we did, they would… "kill" us! Of course, this meant they would beat us up so badly, that we would wish we were dead!

After the patterns of torment had been established, intimidation was employed to abscond our homework. Yes, threatening us with the typical physical abuse was more than enough to coerce us to deliver our Science homework for subsequent copying. This was difficult enough to accept, considering the concerted effort we twins dedicated to our homework assignments, yet sometimes it got even worse. After copying the homework, the bully would hold it in front of us. As we reached for it, he would pull it away, laughing all the while. Then after multiple unsuccessful attempts at retrieval, the flunky would hold it in both hands and then…crumple it!

The few times that the bullies stole our homework without asking and returned it unharmed, was certainly preferable. With our homework now crumpled into a wadded paper ball and our resolution crushed with it, a new fear replaced the prior. How, we wondered, were we going to explain this to our Science teacher? Also, how much would our grade suffer. We could not tell the teacher or our parents lest we get beat-up!

We twins were good students and Mr. Kulczycki was aware that this was not the typical appearance of our homework. After a few occurrences, he confronted Stanley about this one day, calling him forward and asking him for an explanation. Stanley could not speak! He did not know what to say. He stood their shaking. Our experienced and perceptive Science teacher immediately deduced the situation, thankfully. Stanley was not revealed "squealing" and still received proper credit for his homework.

Mr. Kulczycki began keeping a keen eye on which flunky had a homework paper similar to the twin's and eventually the bullies quit stealing and copying our homework.

As we write this story, it is difficult to convey just how skinny and small we were. One episode may give you a clearer picture. Cleave Chime (not his real name), was an older boy who had been held back academically, at least once, maybe twice. One day Chime, in contrast to other days, did not hit us. He instead, demanded that one of us lay sideways on the bench. Stephen, always braver than Stanley, and more willing to endure the harassment himself than witness Stanley being tortured, "volunteered?" So frightened of what physical pain may ensue, Stephen laid sideways, still as a corpse. He silently prayed that his corpse-like stillness was not a premonition.

Anticipating the worse, Stephen closed his eyes. Suddenly, with one swift motion, Chime grabbed him and lifted him into the air. All of the other boys in the room stopped readying themselves for gym, turned and stared at the spectacle before them. Encouraged by the other bullies, with no classmates daring to come to his defense, and with NO gym teacher to be found in the local ZIP CODE, Chime lifted Stephen like a barbell and began "repetitions" with him. Stephen was scarred, not only of Chime, but of being dropped on the unforgiving concrete floor below. Stanley was as helpless to assist as a toothpick in a tornado, but if his internal rage could have been channeled upon Stephen's assailant, Chime would have been dead. We loved one another, but were so physically limited that we were simply unable to help the other.

Both of us were embarrassed. Emboldened by laughter, the muscle-bound bully, Chime, continued till he completed his "workout." After what seemed an eternity, he finally put Stephen down. Fortunately no real physical pain occurred this day, just the psychological pain of humiliation and degradation, perpetuating our feelings of helplessness and insecurity. Worst of all, there were no authorities paying attention, let alone coming to our assistance.

You may read this and simply reject our story as nothing more than "normal" locker room, middle school behavior. You could assume that, but you would be wrong. It was the WORST of times. We endured verbal insults about our pre-pubescent, late maturing bodies, and heard words that shocked our naïve ear drums. The mean-spirited verbal abuse was bad enough, yet we could have survived it, and it alone. However, the raw physicality was almost too much to bear. As we write about it, 40+ years later, our chests collectively tighten, our teeth grit, and our blood pressure rises. It is now obvious, that WE were adversely affected forever by these preventable events.

The bullies continued this pattern of behavior throughout our entire seventh grade year. In fact, our suffering continued/re-occurred again during our eighth grade year, but to a lesser, yet still unacceptable degree.

To this day, we are unsure why Phys. Ed class was a required course. We twins certainly received exponentially more exercise by riding our Schwinn stingray bicycles on our hilly West Virginia neighborhood streets, or shooting basketball on the Ohio Avenue blacktop court, or playing "touch" football in some friend's back yard. We both agree, gym class was a waste of time. Nowadays, if the parents were enlightened about behavior such as this, a "harassment" suit would be filed against the older bullies, and a "dereliction of duty" suit against the gym teacher. Later, in high school, we were cordial and friendly with this teacher, but below the surface, we seethed at his irresponsibility. He failed to protect those of us who could not protect ourselves. Un-American and unbelievable, he had enabled the bullies behavior, not prevented it!

In spite of this neglectful teacher and brutal bullies, we persevered. We credit our friendly dispositions and affable personalities to our loving and nurturing family, and the positive influence of many exceptional adults. Our many "good" childhood experiences outweighed the few "bad" ones, and we evolved without harboring bitterness nor malice toward our fellow man. Though the emotional scars still remain four decades later, our only true wish is that the entire circumstance could have been different during this seventh grade gym class, when our only goal was...*SURVIVAL*.

Slim Twins

Stevie and Stanley, though always skinny and small, were actually cute when they were very young. This is verified by referencing the photograph from the cover of our first book. From year one through kindergarten we might be described as huggable. However, when we got a little taller we became even skinnier, and it was all down hill from there.

Through young adulthood, both of us took comments about our weight, or lack of it, personally. If you look at some of our early photographs you can see why. For all of our childhood, teenage years, and as young adults, we were very thin. Skinny, slim, scrawny, slender, skeleton, skin & bones, brittle, puny, lanky, sickly, gaunt, gangly, bony, dinky, frail, thin, twiggy, and toothpick were all derogatory terms used to describe us. The ridicule was demeaning and hurtful. Some adults even added superlatives to the adjectives when describing us, using terms such as "painfully" thin! Painfully?

For whom? For "them" the observer, or "we" the observed?

Our grade school classmate, empathetic kindred spirit, and fellow friend in frailness, Sherry Lister, probably endured much the same fate. The only positive for us, is that at least we had each other to share the indignation. The famous phrase "misery loves company," certainly applied in our case. Even if WE had been born as just one child instead of twins, the one would have still been below average size!

There are certain photographs of our youthful selves that we look at and cringe. We both become uncomfortable at what appears to be an almost emaciated pair. There is no doubt that we were "picky" eaters as youngsters, but we did not have a diagnosed eating disorder. So worried that there must be a reason for our excessive thinness, Dad, the ever consummate Pharmacist, periodically would instruct us to be "de-wormed." He assumed we must have tapeworms or pinworms living inside us, absorbing all our ingested nutrients. So, about once a year or so, throughout grade school, Dad brought home the "worm" medicine from his Pharmacy. We swallowed six pills each. This medication probably fulfilled its pharmacologically intended purpose, but, of course, it did not alter our basic genetics and thus we remained skinny. We weighed 60 lbs. midway through 6th grade!

Though our lack of body mass was consistently a detriment to us, once a year, it became quite an asset; the annual "penny a pound" promotion at Benedum airport. Dad certainly got his money's worth on this deal. We were so lightweight that the airport authorities put us on the scale and weighed us together. Think about it. In fourth grade, Dad shelled out an entire dollar so we twins could both take a plane ride. It was beneficial not to be "normal" in this instance.

Grandma, Irene Stanley (our Mom's Mother), loved us so, but had an annoying habit of always comparing us to our "normal" size cousins, Bruce and Jeff. We admired how our Grandma had the ability to peel an apple in one continuous piece, and no one could create a flower arrangement quite like her, but we sure wish she would quit reminding us about our gauntness. She would say, "They are so skinny Evelyn, maybe they should see a Doctor. Bruce and Jeff aren't like this. Of course they eat so well in comparison."

Grandma was especially concerned about our narrow heads. She placed her hands on the side of our heads, partially covering our ears and exclaimed, "Their faces are just too flat!" Once, after placing one hand on our jaw and one behind our head and pushing toward one another, she instructed us to no longer sleep on the side of our head at night. She said that that laying our cheeks against the pillow was making our heads too thin.

Not wanting to disappoint Grandma, we both specifically remember going to bed, lying flat on our backs, with heads straight, eyes starring at the gray metal ceiling, and concentrating to stay positioned like this. We hoped that we would wake up in the same position and as a result, maybe our heads might look more normal, like those of our cousins. Of course, it did not work. Genetics ruled once again and our heads remained narrow and "flat," much to Grandma's displeasure. (Let us state for clarification purposes, that the Flat Stanley phenomenon that swept the grade schools throughout the United States in recent years was NOT inspired by Stanley. Though he does bear quite a resemblance to the famous two dimensional figure.)

Long hair was "in" during the early seventies. Dad refused to let us have long hair like all of the other kids, and our very short hair made us appear nerdy. In fact, every time our hair would begin to grow over our ears, Dad made us a barber shop appointment and we were forced to have our hair cut. Our short hair caused our ears and subsequently us, to "stand out," even more than being homely and identical!

During the summer between eighth and ninth grade, Dad finally acquiesced and we grew long hair and "fit in" better. Though Dad says he just became tired of arguing with us, we believe he came to the conclusion that he would rather have good kids that looked bad vs. bad kids that looked good! Looking back at our photographs from that time period, the "cool" long hair just made both of us appear slimmer yet. Long hair remained popular throughout our college days.

In middle school, we both were on the basketball team, but in all honesty, should not have been. We were terrible and obviously had no physicality about us at all. Coach Slinlor (not his real name), a decidedly younger man than his octogenarian appearance would suggest, must have kept us on the team just for laughs. He issued to us, the oldest satin gym shorts available that were a minimum of 10 times too big. Think "Twiggy" in "Fat Albert" shorts. Thank goodness we never got in a game. During practice, Coach Slinlor usually did not involve us with the "real" players. On rare occasion, he might summon us, by the crude nickname he created, "Tampax twins!" This derogatory sobriquet had everyone laughing at our expense. Naive, for quite awhile, we were unaware of its demeaning nature. Once enlightened, we came to resent it, and the older boys that perpetuated the slur.

We were so thin and small, that after one "away" game, Coach Slinlor instructed us to get in the back of his pick-up truck. No big deal you might think. Well, think again! He put the tailgate down and told us to crawl underneath the bed cover! He was in a hurry and would not roll it back. He said we were so skinny that we could easily fit, and he was correct. So, after climbing in, he closed the tailgate and drove off with us lying flat, in the dark, in the back of his Datsun (Pre-Nissan era) pick-up! All of the "real" players had seats in someone's vehicle. We twins, on the other hand, shared the dim and dingy, covered truck bed space with what you might consider standard fare for a pick-up truck: ropes, a few bricks, a tool box, two cinder blocks, oil stained gloves, some trash, a shovel, a rake, a lot of dirt, some grease stained rags, a chain, some loose and rusted nuts and bolts, etc. We were able to see these items only because of our close proximity to them. It was very dark. If only there had been a flashlight, we may have been less anxious….then again, upon reflection, maybe we would have been even more anxious!

The road noise was irritating and the exhaust fumes were nauseating. To "sit" during the basketball game was fair, but to "not sit" on the drive home was demeaning. He drove us back to Nutter Fort in this extremely awkward fashion. After enduring these uncomfortable conditions, our metal house seemed warm and inviting that winter night.

As an adult, Stanley shaves with Gillette Slim Twins razors. Each time he re-opens the pack to retrieve a new razor, he believes Gillette should pay the Toompas twins royalties, because WE were the original...*Slim Twins*.

Sex

Okay, so admit it, after scanning the chapter titles in the Table of Contents, you turned here first! Well, we regret to inform you that this story will not be as titillating as what you have come to expect in this, the second decade of the 21st century. It will however, explain and expose (pun intended) more nuances of our lives.

For those contemporaries that are more prudish, and just cannot believe that Stevie and Stanley would include such a story in their book, do not fret. You will find this chapter to be more akin to "Safe Sex" than "Sex."

As young teens, we twins significantly lagged the other boys in our class developmentally. We hit puberty late. Along with our skinny physiques, this too caused us to be the object of ridicule and explains our seemingly perpetual naiveté. Sometime during 8th grade, 1971-1972, we befriended a classmate named Ray Kools (not his real name.) We were just about to be introduced to a "new world."

We actually became friends with Ray via our math teacher Mrs. Compton. We twins were grasping the 8th grade math concepts easily, but Ray not so well. She asked us to help him in math and we agreed. Ray came over to our house to study some evenings or sometimes we would ride our bikes to his house and assist in arithmetic.

After a few weeks of tutoring, some results were obvious and some were not so obvious. The intended consequence; Ray's math grade improved dramatically. The unintended consequence; Stanley and Stephen were introduced to some different and more pleasing "figures." Yes, this new friendship was enlightening, but as you will soon see, more so for us than for him.

While studying at Ray's house, we discovered that his older brother had a bedroom full of rock and roll posters, lava lamps, a big stereo, hanging strands of beads, and "black" lights mounted throughout. He had albums of Janis Joplin, Jimmy Hendrix and the Doors. We twins had singles with *Chewy, Chewy* by the Ohio Express or *Goody Goody Gumdrops* by the 1910 Fruit Gum Company. We also faithfully watched "The Monkees" on TV. We also remember riding our stingray bikes with an AM radio strapped to the handle bars listening to *Build Me Up Buttercup* by The Foundations. Recently we had begun listening to 3 Dog Night and The Grassroots, but needless to say, we were unaware of FM, Woodstock, and the sexual revolution.

One evening, after completing our math assignment at Ray's house, he closed his bedroom door, opened a dresser drawer to its full extent, stretched and reached behind it, and pulled out some hidden papers. Folded magazine papers. He unfolded them to reveal some things all new to us naive Toompas twins; Pictures featuring those of the opposite sex who were scantily clad!

Over the next few months, Ray revealed many other clandestine locations scattered throughout the local community, all harboring XXX photographs! One secret hiding place was the roofing-shingle sided storage building adjacent to the high school gym. Once while riding bikes up the alley behind Roosevelt-Wilson High School, he skidded to a stop, jumped off his bike, extended his right arm behind a piece of siding, and extracted more photos of scintillating sensations.

On another occasion, we were riding bikes near the parking lot of the swimming pool. This was the off season, so the pool was closed. We parked our bikes in the parking lot and proceeded onto city property. We approached a stack of discarded lumber with tall grass growing all around it. Ray kneeled and reached his hand into the pile. We remember one of his eyebrows raised in a questioning fashion as he searched. Then a smile dominated his face when he realized his hand contacted the intended target that could not be visualized. His hand surfaced with magazines, "adult" magazines, full of buxom beauties and curvaceous cuties.

We suppose that riding bikes around Nutter Fort with Ray was sort of like a pubescent male's treasure hunt from heaven. We did have other adventures, like the time we snuck into the grade school late one evening through the cafeteria door that had been left slightly ajar. Obviously, that stealth and inconsequential enterprise pales in comparison.

Another friend, Moe Hayes (not his real name), was over visiting us one day near the end of 8th grade. Our Mom left to pick up Dad from work. As soon as she left, Moe asks, "Where is your Dad's stash?" We clueless twins wondered what he meant. "You know," he said, "His Playboy magazines." Bewildered we shook our heads conveying doubt. Unconvinced, Moe took four steps from our bedroom into our parents' bedroom, asked which set of drawers were our Father's, and then proceeded, ignoring our objections, to open Dad's top drawer.

Searching momentarily and ever so superficially, Moe discovered a Playboy magazine. We were shocked. We asked Moe, "How in the world did he know our Dad had a Playboy." He replied with authority, "ALL Dad's have them!" He enjoyed the magazine for what seemed like an eternity. Finally he replaced it, our parent's arrived home about 30 seconds later, Moe left, and our paradigm had shifted.

Undetected(?), we "visited" the drawer on those rare occasions that neither parent was home, though we did not yet comprehend the pleasing nature of the pictures. For years, Stanley related this story differently, as if Dad had caught us with the Playboy magazine. Stanley reports that Dad sternly lectured us saying, "If you boys continue to read that filth and smut, you'll go blind!" Stanley deftly replies, "But Dad ... We're over here!"

All joking aside, it seems obvious to us now, that boys such as Ray and Moe, who had reached puberty earlier, were probably "driven crazy" by it. No wonder Ray could not do well in junior high classes, sexual thoughts probably dominated him. No doubt, he had a difficult time concentrating, especially, since there was a girl in our 8th grade class that must have been Dolly Pardon's identical twin sister!

For sake of completion, you should know that our Father did try to have a "serious," sit-down discussion about the "birds and the bees" which turned out disastrous. With our cardigan-sweater clad Dad in his recliner and we twins on the couch, he presented his "sex" talk. Embarrassed, we remember laughing and giggling the entire time and comprehending very little relevant information. Dad was incredulous. He had miscalculated our readiness for such a dissertation because of some forbidden words he had overheard us using. He abruptly halted his sex lecture and said, "If you boys already think you know everything about sex we can end this discussion now." It ended immediately, but as you have already discovered, we twins knew nothing.

After puberty finally engulfed us also, Stanley remembers distinctly sitting in Miss Lindsey's 9th grade American Studies class and being oddly attracted to her on certain days? Also, he remembers purposely dropping a pencil multiple times to allow himself to turn slightly and look backwards upon retrieval. This offered him a "bird's eye" view of a "developed," mini-skirt clad, freshman girl's legs. Stanley was still confused as to why he was compelled to do this. He felt much like a remote controlled vehicle. Testosterone is a powerful drug!

At the time, our favorite Rock and Roll band was The Raspberries, featuring Eric Carmen. After the onset of puberty, their songs such as, *Go All The Way, Ecstasy, I Wanna Be With You, Let's Pretend,* and *Tonight*, added to our teenage angst! In 1974, we had the opportunity to see the "Raspberries" in concert at the Nathan Goff Armory in Clarksburg, West Virginia, with the band "Looking Glass," famous for the song *Brandy*.

So, for we twins, the late onset of puberty was a detriment when it came to our physicality, as chronicled in our story "Survival." However with hind sight 20/20 (Stanley, the Optometrist, loves to use this phrase), it may have been a blessing in disguise. We had a prolonged childhood compared to others. We could concentrate on our schoolwork, enjoy being kids, and not yet be distracted by...*Sex*.

Cleaning Shelves

As youngsters, we twins probably had Attention Deficit Disorder, as we have always been hyper. Our Dad probably sought to improve our concentration abilities when he suggested that we clean shelves at Bland's Drug store for a few weeks in the summer. Not thrilled at first, Dad enticed us by offering $1 per hour, and, although not contractually agreed upon, all the Lance peanut butter and cheese crackers we could eat. In the early 70's, this was incentive enough. As we will explain, this job may have cured us of ADD (Attention Deficit Disorder), but induced OCD (Obsessive Compulsive disorder.) So, while other kids were at the city pool getting tanned, we were indoors attempting to make pharmacy shelves as white as we were.

Though we cleaned every shelf in the entire drug store one summer, the main concern were the ones in the pharmacy that contained the prescribed pharmaceuticals. First, we cleaned the floor in front of the shelves, then we placed all items from the bottom shelf onto the floor, in the exact order and position that we removed them.

This process was crucial, as these important substances were stored in alphabetical order and Dad was working and using the inventory as we cleaned. We scrubbed all surfaces of the shelf and wiped them dry. We then repeated the exact same mind-numbing procedure for the next shelf, and the next, and the next, *ad nauseum. (*our high school Latin teacher would have appreciated this, and so would've Dad!) We used a stepladder to gain access to the high shelves. Once we finished an entire section, it was time to reverse the process and replace all medications to their original positions, shelf by monotonous shelf.

Even with two to tackle the job, this painstaking process seemed to take "forever." The discipline needed to complete the task probably benefited us greatly. We twins had a lawn mowing service, but it had defined limits and was completed in a relatively short time frame. This job took many weeks and seemed as though it would never ever end.

We were introduced to numerous medication names, manufacturer's names, and learned a lot by handling the bottles. We actually delighted in the variety of medications and marveled at the various bottle shapes and packaging. At the time, the majority of medications were in glass containers, so we had to be very careful and cautious. We are proud to report that we had a perfect cleaning record as we had no glass bottles break, ever!

One time Stephen got a stomach ache while working. Possibly he ate too many cheese crackers. Dad instructed him to take a Zantac, but he accidentally took a Zanex instead! His stomach still hurt…but he didn't care! (Sorry. Stanley coerced Stephen to place some "Pharmacy" humor in the text. This is an obvious joke as it constitutes an anachronism, since these medications had not yet been invented.) Stanley sure hopes that he didn't make a "spectacle" of himself when including this joke in the text. (Sorry again, but Stanley just loves the Optometric humor also, and is not shy about using it.)

Once in a while, Dad would give us a break from the monotony of cleaning shelves, by sending us on a mission to another drug store to retrieve a medication that Bland's was lacking. His only instructions were to get it quickly, quietly and safely. Stanley and Stephen loved these covert excursions.

Back in the 60's and 70's, there were many small drug stores in Clarksburg besides Bland's. Within two city blocks were Mercer's, Wells-Haymaker, Harbert's and Byard's Pharmacies. Our errands usually took place in the evening hours and we treated each one as a sort of a reconnaissance mission. Sneaking around parked cars, hiding behind lamp posts, or parking meters (remember we were thin); we traveled stealthily toward our destination. If only we would have had our walkie-talkies with us!

Upon arriving at the appropriate location, the pharmacist at the competitor's store was always happy to see Ed's twins and treated us respectfully. We would return to Bland's in a less circuitous route after we had accomplished the mission. Dad was always well pleased. Then we returned to our shelf cleaning chores.

This job gave us even greater respect for our Father. We watched him work an often times stressful Pharmacy counter, yet interact joyfully with customers. He knew everything about a myriad of prescribed medications, and a multitude of the "over the counter" variety. He dispensed not only drugs, but advice, similar to a Physician. He was smart. We thought that he was incredible. As teenagers, we always felt that if we could eventually be just half as intelligent and could develop just half of his personality, we would be quite successful in life. Since we are identical twins, we do believe that we each indeed got just about half!

For sake of completion, we will inform you that Dad was also very active in his profession. He served as President of the WV Pharmaceutical Association in 1981 and was voted outstanding Alumnus of the year in 1973. He was instrumental in establishing mandatory continuing education for West Virginia Pharmacists, and spearheaded the restructuring of the externship program at the WVU School of Pharmacy. Along with his business associates, we endowed a scholarship in his name at the West Virginia University School of Pharmacy upon his death in 1994.

We have fond memories of our time spent at Bland's Drug Store, whether it was visiting or working. We were enriched by our experiences there.

Perhaps Dad realized the information garnered, the lessons learned and the value gained while...*Cleaning Shelves*.

{Special note: Stephen works at Town and Country Drug Store, but also co-owns Michael's Pharmacy in West Union, Village Pharmacy in Lost Creek, and Colonial Drug Store in Salem. It is difficult to announce, but as of this writing (7/11/11), Bland's has been closed.}

Chess Kings

Due to the complexities of life and the multitude of problems facing America, yet the helplessness we feel when pondering it all, Stanley is fond of repeating this insightful analogy, "We are just pawns on the chessboard of life." Profound, huh?

Well in 2012 perhaps, we twins are just pawns, but it was different a long time ago. In fact, in the early to mid 70's we twins were kings. Chess Kings.

We were introduced to the game as children, watching our Dad and Uncle Everett playing with a Renaissance style chess set, in our dining room of our metal house. We observed, interrupted, and learned.

As we grew older, we twins would wake up on a Saturday morning, eat a bowl of Frosted Flakes or Rice Krispies, and play a game of chess. We sat on the floor and placed the board on the ebony inlayed blond coffee table. One odd memory about those times that stands out, is that one of us would make his move and while the other waited, he would scratch his head. The air in the metal house had low humidity which made our scalps itch. By the time check mate was reached, our ebony table top appeared ivory with a white dusting of disgusting dandruff!

As we twins began 9th grade, Uncle Everett encouraged us to join the school's chess club. Reluctantly, and with great consternation, we gathered enough courage and followed his advice. Good move (pun intended.)

Throughout our childhood, Uncle Everett always "flipped" a quarter to each of us whenever he visited, which secured us quite a bounty at Gin's Pick-up. The money was a short term gain, but his encouragement to play the game of chess was infinitely more beneficial, with positive long term ramifications. Virtues gained or enhanced by the chess matches we played included: better concentration, more patience, improved sequential memory capabilities, endurance, mental toughness, and sometimes "holding your bladder," but we digress.

Chess, always a metaphor for war with two opposing kingdoms, reached it's all-time, worldwide height in popularity in the early 1970's, corresponding perfectly with the cold war. Ironically enough, chess enthusiasm peaked with the World Championships played between representatives of those cold war participants, Boris Spasky of the Soviet Union, and Bobby Fisher of the United States. Taking place from July through September of 1972, this was an absolute "classic" chess match and represented almost perfect symbolism for the times; East vs. West, Communism vs. Democracy, Socialism vs. Capitalism, USSR vs. USA.

High school chess club was the only extra-curricular activity in which we twins participated during our Freshman year. Mr. Hart, our English teacher, served as our advisor. He was a good teacher as well as a very good chess player. Many of the academically motivated and intellectual students played chess. Association with these smarter and older students benefited us greatly. We even began beating our Father on a consistent basis! During that Freshman year, our high school team finished #6 of 40+ teams at the State Chess Tournament.

By the time we were juniors, we had already represented Roosevelt-Wilson in numerous competitions and became officers in the club. As with athletic endeavors, a chess player only improves by playing those ranked higher and considered better. We did and won often. During our sophomore and junior years, we represented Roosevelt-Wilson High School in the West Virginia State Chess Tournament in Charleston. We helped the school to another top 10 finish at #10 as sophomores. During our junior year, Stanley played well and made the All-Tournament team (4 wins, 1 draw, 1 loss), the chess equivalent to All-State status. However, the team finished a still respectful but disappointing 15th place.

Truth be known, Stephen was probably the better player and beat Stanley more often than not. Stephen took a pragmatic approach to the game and due to his familiarity with Stanley's strategies, or lack thereof, trumped him often. However, when pitted against players from other high schools, especially at the state chess tournament, Stanley's unique unorthodoxy led to many a victory over flummoxed opponents.

Early in our junior year, our team participated in a chess tournament at Lewis County High School. Stephen was awesome on this day. A four game competition, Stephen was one of only two players to emerge unscathed after three games. The tournament director approached him and invited him to table #1 to play the only other undefeated, 3-0 player, a home-standing Lewis County student, for the tournament championship. Stephen reached out his hand to greet his competitor, but the fellow refused tradition. Instead, the boy points his finger toward the sign on the table that displays a large "#1" and says to Stephen, "I collect these!" Stephen was instantly intimidated. Even though the chess pieces were black and white, this was certainly not an example of Paul McCartney/Stevie Wonder's *Ebony and Ivory* living in perfect harmony moment!

Methodical in his approach, and gallant in his effort, Stephen nonetheless wilted under the pressure induced by the more experienced and seasoned opponent. It also did not help Stephen's cause, that the long match drew observers who gathered around the table to view the tournament championship, after the conclusion of their own abbreviated matches. This added to the palpable tension that caused him to make a crucial error late in the game. As it became obvious that Stephen would loose, the crowd dispersed. Stephen subsequently lost and reluctantly accepted a very admirable second place finish for the tournament.

Beyond high school competitions, we played in events sanctioned by the United States Chess Federation. Stanley actually achieved a respectable USCF ranking. For three years we played a lot of chess. So much so that we were "burned out" by our senior year. After becoming club officers again, our hearts just were not in it and we deferred to the younger players. Many good players that had motivated us had graduated the previous year. Also, Stanley's responsibilities as Student Body President took precedence. We quit playing chess competitively halfway through that senior year in high school, our other activities having literally put us in "check mate."

Sad to report, but Uncle Everett, who had been our original mentor and motivator, died in 1973, a few months after urging us to join the high school chess club. We are sure that he would have been proud of our successes. We thank him for the chance to reign, if only for a short time, as...*Chess Kings*.

The President's President

    We both had wonderful high school experiences. We are well aware that not all Americans can say that, and do consider ourselves quite fortunate. Our high school was a median sized West Virginia high school, supported by the surrounding community of Nutter Fort, and accountable to it. We have fond memories of this place. It was called Roosevelt-Wilson, and like The White House in DC, was appropriately situated on Pennsylvania Ave. It was named after Theodore Roosevelt (R) the 26th President, and Woodrow Wilson (D), the 28th President. (We always wondered what happened to Taft?) The school's nickname was the Presidents or Prexies, and the school colors were Red and Gray. The first graduating class was in 1926. We twins, along with 126 classmates, would be part of the 50th, and it would correspond with the nation's bicentennial.

    Though no longer serving as a high school, the building is still proudly standing. It is over 85+ years old! Many school buildings have been built, used, and subsequently torn down during that time. We maintain, to this day, that if there was a nuclear missile attack, the basement of this building would be the safest place to be on the planet!

We twins studied hard, liked our teachers, were academically successful, and graduated as co-Salutatorians in 1976, along with Sheila Bond. We took our lessons seriously from the very beginning. We both did well on the ACT test (i.e. 30 of 32 in Math), and even attended a summer symposium in Science and Engineering at Case Western Reserve University in Cleveland Ohio in the summer of 1975, along with Chuck Bray. We were each honored as "Boy of the Month" our senior year because of our good academics and the many extra-curricular activities in which we participated. We were very involved in our school…but it did not begin that way for the Toompas twins.

Just in case the previous text paints us as somewhat narcissistic to you, let us assure you that it was necessary, so to preface the following—in stark contrast to the way it ended, we began high school as semi-recluses!

The junior high occupied the basement of the building, and the high school the top two floors. We are quite sure that if we had not been awkward appearing identical twins, no one would have noticed us emerging from the basement as we began high school. To "fit in" and be as inconspicuous as possible, our hair was long, we wore platform shoes, hand-me down shirts from our cousins, Bruce and Jeff, and bell-bottom pants purchased at the "Threads Ahead" department of The Workingman's Store in Clarksburg. The wider the bell bottom, the "cooler" the pants. In fact the coolest boys at the high school had "elephant bells" or colorful, excess material sewed into the pant leg bottoms to make them even wider! Straight leg pants were nerdy in the 1970's.

Our entire freshman and sophomore years were dominated almost exclusively by academics. The only extra-curricular activities we undertook were the Chess Club and then the Leo Club our sophomore year. We twins did attend some varsity football games, and we were ardent fans of the 1972-73 and the 1973-74 RW basketball teams that made the 4-team AA state tournament, which was quite an accomplishment considering this was before school consolidation became rampant. Usually however, we were home studying. At the end of our sophomore year, everything changed.

Stanley takes the story solo from here:

To many of you reading this and to many of you 50+ years old, high school may seem a trite, distant and inconsequential memory. Not so with me. I relish my experiences there and enjoyed the overall high school ambiance. As stated, the official Roosevelt-Wilson school "colors" were Red and Grey. As of this writing, my wife, Kim (RW, class of '80), and I own two vehicles, one red and the other gray! I guess it is still in my blood 36 years after graduating. Here is why:

Near the end of 10th grade, we twins were standing by our locker at the end of a long day, gathering our thoughts and our books, eager to go home. All of a sudden, I got a tap on my shoulder. I turned around to face Elaine George. She was a bespectacled senior, popular, very pretty, and one of the most intelligent students at our high school, and I nervously wondered what she wanted with me.

Then it happened. It was the seminal moment in my life. Elaine urged me to run for student council office and that she wanted to be my campaign manager! I was dumbfounded. Me? Unbelievable! What now, in hind sight, seems inconceivable, I then asked her, "What is student council?" That is just how uninvolved and unaware we twins were up to this point in high school. She explained everything. Then I asked, "Why me?" She said that student council needed a "regular" guy to run. Someone with no ego, nor pretense, just a common, decent kid. Wow, did I feel special at that moment. (Thinking back, I wonder if it was just by luck that she tapped me on the shoulder vs. Stephen. Had she been the rare entity that discerned our differences and actually decided upon me? I doubt it.)

I soon agreed to her offer, and just could not believe my good fortune. I was running for Vice-President of the student body, and the 1974 Salutatorian and homecoming princess had volunteered to be my campaign manager. Had I died and gone to heaven? Win or loose, my world had just changed forever.

Thanks to Elaine's encouragement, efforts, ideas and inspiration, I won the election for Vice-President and thoroughly enjoyed the experience. (By the way, Stephen ran for Treasurer and lost). While looking through some old scrapbooks recently, I found some handbills that I passed out to students when campaigning. One handbill, believe it or not, was in the shape of eyeglasses! (Foreshadowing? Quite possibly, but as usual, I digress!) The election process greatly boosted our meager self-esteems. During our junior year, we were not only involved with student council, but also Leo Club, Thespians, Chess Club, Science Club, and the Junior class play.

I represented the student council at the sports boosters club meetings, and originated a Red & Grey toboggan (or "ski cap" to the known world beyond West Virginia) sold locally.

I would be remiss if I did not mention the student council sponsored student exchange that year. This will be of interest because it involves our cousin Jeff (reference "Scouting Report" from our first book.)

The most intense competitor for our high school was crosstown rival, WI (Washington-Irving High School.) So heated had the RW-WI rivalry become, that both student councils decided to have a student exchange to foster good will. I represented RW at WI and attended classes. After making my self comfortable in an English class, I was surprised to see my cousin Jeff. I knew Jeff was a nonconformist, but on this day he repeatedly made some disrupting noise which constantly interrupted the teacher. Embarrassed because of the guests present in her class room, the teacher announced to Jeff, that if he did not cease and desist, he would have to leave the classroom. I turned to look at Jeff. He paused, gave the teacher a quizzical look, stated loudly, "Don't mind if I do" and defiantly left the classroom. I did not see him again for the remainder of my exchange visit. (Note: I am told that as a teenager, Jeff may have attended high school every day, but did not attend many classes.

Ironically, Jeff became a teacher. He has taught and coached at University High School in Morgantown for many years. He is a well-respected, good Christian man and I am proud to be related to him.) The student exchange was deemed a success nonetheless.

At the end of our junior year, Stephen and I were both selected for Mountaineer Boys State and inducted into The National Honor Society. My concerted effort with student council enabled us twins to evolve and safely exist without the other glued to his hip. We twins began developing our own unique personalities and become more of an individual rather than a collective unit.

With our junior year nearing its end and my new found confidence in hand, I decided to run for Student Council President. Dan McKiernan, 1975 Salutatorian, graciously decided to serve as my campaign manager.

With Stephen's help, we placed posters around the school with such slogans as, "Toompas or not Toompas, that is the question?," "Snoopy says, Vote for Toompy" (This was definitely foreshadowing, as you will discover in the next story "Twins, Taught a Lesson"), and "Stan the Man has the Plan."

I campaigned hard. It seems as though I talked to every student, many by telephone in the evenings. We even had a parade, approved by Principle Lindy Bennett, around the school the day before the election. It consisted of three cars with signs plastered on the sides. Leading the parade was our white 1974 Ford Pinto, driven by Stephen. Next was a green 1958 Chevy driven by our friend Bernie Maze. Bringing up the rear was a 1962 black Corvair convertible driven by our childhood buddy, Eddie Bee, with me, the candidate, sitting up in the back waving in the open air. In the end, all the effort paid off and I won the election. It is still one of the happiest moments and best memories of my entire life.

I served my senior year with fellow student council officers, George Mancini, Teena Medina and Bill Hoover. We attended summer student council camp at West Virginia Wesleyan College where we met future West Virginia Governor and current US. Senator, Jay Rockefeller. Our student council advisor was the assistant principle, Mr. Skidmore, who guided us prudently. We had an active student government and even held open student council meetings for the entire student body to attend. We purchased new water fountains to replace some half-century old ones that no longer worked. We put clocks in every classroom. We even erected a large scoreboard in front of RWHS displaying the varsity football results. We operated a book store during the late summer in the school's basement.

I had a blast serving as student body president and surmised that I was on top of the world. I felt needed and important. At times, at home, my Father believed me to be belligerent. Maybe I was becoming a "real" politician?

I truly never wanted it to end.

Time does pass however, schools consolidate, and everything changes. Ironically, the longtime rivals, the Roosevelt-Wilson Presidents and the Washington Irving Hilltoppers combined to form the Robert C Byrd Flying Eagles High School in the 1990's (Isn't going from 2 Presidents to one Senator a step down?) Also, I am 53 years old as I write this story, I can honestly say that the student council is not only responsible for many good things that happened to me in high school, but also, for many good things that happened to me in my adult life. It boosted my self-confidence, introduced me to public speaking and speech writing, indwelt me with a spirit of service, improved my organizational skills, and opened many doors of opportunity for me.

Even though it may seem to the reader as overstated, I am sincere to my core: Elaine George altered my future and changed me forever. About ten years ago, I was able to procure her phone number. Even though I was in my 40's at the time, I was anxious while dialing the phone and nervous when talking to her. Almost, how one would feel when in close proximity to a celebrity. A quarter of a century had passed, but I finally said, "Thank You" to Elaine George. My life would not have been as enjoyable and I would not have been nearly as successful, if not for her and the opportunity and subsequent privilege to serve as...*The President's President*.

{Special note: Coincidentally, as this chapter was being written, Stanley's daughter followed in her Father's footsteps and was elected as Student Council President of Philip Barbour High School, in Barbour County, West Virginia, for the 2011-12 school year. By the time this book is published, she will have completed her term. We hope she enjoyed it as much as her Father did.}

I'm The One The Other Isn't-Book Two

Twins, Taught a Lesson

We were fortunate to have had many dedicated and competent teachers at Roosevelt-Wilson High School back in the mid 1970's. They included:

Mr. Kulczycki, Mr. Alvino, Mr. Nesler, Mr. Coffindaffer, Mr. Loretta, Mr. Snider, Mrs. Colombo, Mrs. Smith, Mrs. Maxwell, Ms. Lindsey, Coach Gainer, Mrs. Compton, Mrs. Campbell, Mr. Dolan, Coach Johnson, Ms. Secreta, Mr. Hart, Ms. Jermont, Mrs. Clayton, Mrs. Romano, Mr. Merchant, Mr. Bailey, Mr. Hyre, *et al*. (*Mrs. Robinson, our Latin teacher, would have appreciated this too.) Our ninth grade Algebra teacher is purposely not mentioned here. You can read more about Mrs. Whitener in the chapter, "(Twins + Algebra) x 2 = Stress," included in our first book of Stevie-Stanley Stories. Most of our teachers had a positive influence on our lives and we appreciate their devotedness. Mrs. Hoban, the Librarian was also quite helpful. Mrs. Jean Sullivan served as our Guidance Counselor.

The Principal, Mr. Lindy Bennett, and the Assistant Principle,

Mr. Robert Skidmore, were actually quite young, but provided excellent discipline and leadership. Though not teaching in a classroom, we twins did learn a lot from them.

Mr. Clint Nesler, who taught Algebra Two, and Geometry, was outstanding. Because of Mrs. Paulett Compton, our competent junior high math teacher, we had come to expect good math instruction, and we were not disappointed. He made the class memorize all the Geometry postulates, corollaries and theorems. This exercise alone helped us develop excellent memory capabilities, which in turn, benefited us greatly in college. Our children did not have the same requirements at their respective high schools, much to their detriment. During one six weeks grading period, Stanley missed an "A" by an excruciatingly close margin; accidentally inverting a fraction on one problem on the last test! When Stanley approached Mr. Nesler to complain, he responded, "Yes, I could give you the "A," since you are on the border line, but Stanley, YOU have no business being on the borderline! Since you fell short, you get the "B" you earned." Stanley was really angry for quite a while. However, the ultimate consequence was that Stanley stayed off of all borderlines and never again allowed his fate to rest with the teacher. Our respect for Mr. Nesler grew as the years passed. By the way, we are old, but we did not learn advanced math with a slide rule. We were permitted to use our awesome, new, state-of-the-art Texas Instruments multiple function calculator.

Mr. Aurelio Alvino taught Chemistry, Physics, Trigonometry and Calculus. He was brilliant. He would always remind us that everything is "relative." For example, if we asked him just how big, or heavy, or fast, or dense, or whatever something was, he would answer with a question, "Compared to what?" Chairman of the science department, he presented Stephen with the outstanding senior science award. After high school graduation, Mr. Alvino was also gracious enough to help tutor Stephen with his college calculus class. The man was a truly gifted science and math teacher. We remained friends for many years.

Mrs. Virginia Colombo was our typing teacher. Yes, youngsters, "typing" on a typewriter. Computers and their word processing key boards did not exist yet in the mid 70's. Mrs. Colombo lived directly across the street from the high school. She was an attractive, confident lady who was in command of her classroom. She taught typing. We twins learned typing. The skill has been valuable to us as Stephen uses a keyboard constantly at his pharmacy and Stanley opts to type reports and letters at his office, since no one can read his writing! In fact, while creating our manuscripts for both books, Stanley is "typing" or "keyboarding" not writing, and nearly effortlessly so, thanks to Mrs. Colombo.

Ms. Patricia Lindsey taught American history. She was a recent college graduate who was passionate as well as compassionate. Stanley distinctly remembers her comforting him at the end of an American Studies class in ninth grade, over the loss of our Grandfather. She also directed our Senior class play, "You're a Good Man Charlie Brown," and cast Stanley as Snoopy. This was one of the most enjoyable experiences in his life. Upon audition, she said that Stanley would be perfect for the part of Snoopy, probably because of his long and scraggly hair. He argued that he could not play the part because it required singing! She eased his angst by assuring him that she would personally tutor him and explained, "You do not need to sing perfect Stanley, you're playing the part of a dog!" She was special.

Mr. Vernon Hart recently passed away. We miss him. He served as the Chess Club advisor. We liked him a lot and he was a good English teacher.

During our Freshman English class, he introduced a voluntary "show and tell" week for any student who was inclined to share a hobby or collection.

Stanley and Stephen decided to bring in their entire pop can collection. This collection included about one hundred colorful metal cans. After sharing a unique point about each can and explaining the origin of those from outside the state, we stacked them into a tower like fashion. Upon conclusion, Mr. Hart, a kid at heart (that was cool), then asked if he could knock the entire stack down! We felt obligated to oblige him, and the entire stack came crashing to the floor! The bell rang to indicate the change of classes, and fortunately some incoming students assisted in picking up the scattered cans. Needless to say, we were late for Latin class.

Also, Mr. Hart made learning fun by relating it to our current lives. For example, when he taught the different parts of prose and poetry, he suggested we bring in any "45" rock and roll records that contained examples. Whether it be foreshadowing, metaphor, onomatopoeia, anachronism, idiom, etc., we twins brought some of our "singles" to school. Mr. Hart played them on the record player and commented appropriately.

Mrs. Marjorie Campbell took English to another level. If you approached her as she stood beside her doorway between classes, and happened to engage her in conversation, you had better be grammatically correct. If not, she would pause to allow the student a moment to try and realize his linguistic *faux pas* himself, which would tend to be very embarrassing. Usually squirming and unable to recognize your error, she would admonish you and ameliorate your statement on the spot! At the time, we were most certainly insulted, but years later, we realized that these hallway rendezvous with Mrs. Campbell were quite beneficial. She actually cared.

Though we were inept writers as ninth grade students, we know that Mr. Hart would have enjoyed our current books. Mrs. Campbell may have been tougher to please, but we believe that she too will take pleasure in reading them, albeit with a grin on her face, and a correcting marker in her hand!

As explained in the story "Survival," Mr. Walter Kulczycki was a seventh grade science teacher. He also taught eighth and ninth grade science. He made science exciting for us and built our self-confidence. Extremely intelligent, he was meticulously prepared and organized. Oh yes, we forgot to mention, he was thorough. In ninth grade, he taught the entire science book. Let us repeat that last sentence for emphasis: He taught the ENTIRE science book! And, generation X'ers, this was not an "MTV" Science book, full of politically correct color photographs and large space-occupying diagrams. Our textbook was uniform to a fault, with seemingly infinite text and voluminous vocabulary words. We did it all! For the record we have to report, that for many years, neither Stanley's wife nor his children believed him when he told them about the amount of science he learned. Then two years ago, Stanley found our ninth grade science book and the veracity-proving syllabus inside. Mr. Kulczycki took his job seriously, and taught science. ALL of it!

Coach Del Gainer taught Phys. Ed. and coached both football and baseball. He was a WVU graduate and played for the Mountaineers alongside Jim Braxton. Jim was an excellent running back, kicker and an All-American tight end at West Virginia University in the late 1960's. Jim is more well known as the blocking back for the famous, later infamous, OJ Simpson, while with the Buffalo Bills. Coach Gainer used his influence to convince Jim to present a motivational speech at Roosevelt-Wilson in 1974, at the pinnacle of Jim's career. Great idea by Coach Gainer, and great presentation by Mr. Braxton. Coach Gainer was a fun-loving fellow and a good coach. His 1974 RWHS football team, quarterbacked by All-Stater Randy Gorby, finished ranked 5th in the state in AA and missed the playoffs by .05 points! That was quite an accomplishment since only 4 teams made the playoffs back then!

Neither Stanley or Stephen had a business math class taught by Mrs. Karen Clayton, but we became friends and respected her nonetheless. Stanley had many opportunities to stop by her classroom during his senior year. He would kneel by her desk and engage her in conversation. Mrs. Clayton would learn of the latest student news from the Student Council President, and Stanley would seek much needed advice from a level-headed teacher. In Stanley's high school yearbook, Mrs. Clayton wrote, "You spent more time in my classroom than some of my students."

We really liked Mr. Robert Loretta. He taught American Studies and was a recent graduate who enjoyed teaching. He was conscientious, efficient, and made history interesting. While at the high school, established teachers such as Mr. Donald Dolan, Mr. David Hyre, and the Band Director, Mr. Harry Bailey, supported mustaches. They encouraged Mr. Loretta to grow one too. It wasn't easy. So feeble was the attempt, in fact, that Stanley made jokes about it at assemblies and a "friendly feud" commenced for an entire school year. The student body loved the drama. Funny thing about life, the old saying, "what goes around, comes around" is true. During college, Stephen grew a mustache easily, yet Stanley struggled pathetically. We believe Mr. Loretta had the last laugh.

Mr. Paul Snider taught our shop class (Industrial Arts) in ninth grade and also coached basketball and football at RW. His wife Jackie was employed by Town and Country Drug Store and still works there to this day! Paul was a gentle man and soft-spoken. He exhibited a calm demeanor when teaching shop and everyone liked him. Sad to say, he died unexpectedly in 2002, and is missed by many.

The Thespian advisor was Mr. Donald Dolan. He taught World Culture and English, but neither of us had his class. Mr. Dolan was well-respected and also fun to be around. Truth be known, finally revealed after all these years, Mr. Dolan encouraged and collaborated with Stanley concerning most shenanigans directed at Mr. Loretta!

We could write endlessly about our high school teachers, but that would require an entire book, not just a single chapter within a book. However, we would be remiss if we did not mention Mr. A.L. Coffindaffer. A devoted Biology teacher who also died too young, he too was exceedingly prepared. For a few weeks during sophomore Biology class, Mr. Coffindaffer had a "student teacher" from Glenville State College named Mr. Glenn Righman.

He was baptized by fire, as he had to teach the reproductive chapters to a class full of immature, testosterone laden teenage boys, sitting in a coed classroom!

An avid hunter, young Mr. Righman drove an always dirty, camper-topped pick-up truck to school. One Friday night, after a full week of lectures on the reproductive cycle, sex cells, chromosomes, etc., we became mischievous. On the way home after school, we passed by Mr. Righman's consistently filthy truck and was inspired to display our maturity, or lack thereof, by "writing" in the dust on his vehicle. In large print, at multiple sites, we dubbed his truck, "The Sperm-mobile." We thought this was not only clever, but ultimately hilarious.

Compared to our classmates, we twins were still very naive as sophomores. Christening his vehicle, the "Sperm-mobile," was just clean fun with his dirty truck! By Monday, somehow, Mr. Righman found out it was we twins who defiled his truck. He confronted us, smiled, laughed, and it ended right there. No harm - no foul. A thorough car washing removed all evidence of this harmless yet humorous prank, and the serendipitous result was that Mr. Righman finally had his truck clean for the first time in many months. Just having innocent fun in 1974, the Sperm-mobile disappeared quickly, but the memory remains forever. End of story? Not quite!

Fast-forward 10 years to 1984. Stanley's Optometrist practice was in it's infancy in Philippi. Into the office walks this patient named Sharon. As Stanley extends his hand of welcome, a male voice behind Sharon says, "Be careful honey, do you think this Toompas knows anything yet? It may even be his twin brother standing in for him." Stanley thought the voice sounded familiar but could not place it. Then Mr. Righman emerges into view and instantly Stanley recognized him. Laughter abound. Then Glenn introduced his wife and explained that he currently taught science at the Philippi Middle School. Sharon already knew that the Toompas twins were Glenn's "first" students, and was previously aware of the "Sperm-mobile" story. Of course, Glenn had Stanley re-tell it anyway. A decade old, but still funny.

Somewhere in the early 2000's Stephen met Glenn again, while dining with Stanley in a Morgantown restaurant. Glenn and Sharon were heading out, we twins with our families were heading in. Pleased to see both of us together, after 30 years, Glenn stated that his filthy truck was parked out in the lot, and that he was glad we were unaware of his presence inside the restaurant because, he observed, "Who knows what would be written on the side of my truck this time!" The "Sperm-mobile" legend lived on.

Sharon and Glenn remained Stanley's patients and friends until, like Mr. Coffindaffer, Glenn also met an early and unexpected demise while on a camping trip in 2005. A cruel twist of fate, Mr. Righman died the summer before he was to teach eighth grade science to Stanley's son Chris! Unfortunate, as Glenn was heralded as an outstanding educator. He often repeated that he was looking forward to teaching another Toompas and telling Chris stories about the twins and maybe even the Sperm-mobile! Then, life would have come full-circle and the...*Twins, Taught a Lesson*.

Cruising The Burger Chef

Ask anybody that was familiar with the place, Nutter Fort was a charming small town in the 1960's and early 70's. Juxtaposed to Clarksburg, it was quaint, quiet, and the quintessential American community. Even though our Mandan Road address was designated as Clarksburg, we lived two streets over from Nutter Fort and essentially spent a majority of our youth there. The grade school, high school, park, basketball courts, many friends, Gin's Pick-up, and our family's other Pharmacy, Town and Country Drug Store, had Nutter Fort addresses.

At the time, the Clarksburg/Bridgeport/Nutter Fort area had no world famous fast food restaurants yet. Small, independent, family owned establishments dominated the landscape. The list of our favorite foods and the eateries are as follows:

1) Best hot dogs - Thelma's Lunch [Second best - Bennett's Snack Bar (while listening to *Sugar Sugar* by the Archies on the juke box)]

2) Best doughnuts - Bonnie Belle's (especially twisted glazed)

3) Best Onion Rings, French fries, Hoagies - Parkette (while

listening to the juke box playing, *Hanky Panky*, by Tommy James and the Shondells or *Lady Willpower*, by Gary Puckett and the Union Gap)

    4) Best Soup Beans - West Virginia Restaurant

    5) Best soft serve ice cream - Mr. Alvarez's Dairy Queen

    6) Best hard ice cream - Big Scoop

    7) Best Pizza - Twin Oaks Restaurant (while listening to the Juke Box playing *Band of Gold* by Freda Payne or *Don't Pull Your Love*, by Hamilton, Joe, Frank, and Reynolds) [Second Best: Smitty's Pizza]

    8) Best Hamburger -?

Well, as we have explained earlier, Stevie and Stanley were picky eaters, but one thing we would eat was hamburgers, our Mother's fried hamburgers. We ate so many at home that we chose other options if eating out. Then everything changed. A hamburger mill moved into Nutter Fort only 2 ½ blocks from our house! No, it was not McDonald's, but it was very similar in marketing and menu: hamburgers, bigger hamburgers, fries, carbonated fountain drinks, and milk shakes. Fast food, and at that time, cheap food! We twins loved eating there. It was called Burger Chef.

    The entire facility was made of glass and you could actually view the employees working from any seat in the establishment, or any car in the parking lot for that matter. Multiple booths were present and some really cool orange bar stools lined each side. Ok, so it wasn't McDonald's! Truth be known, we were not even aware of McDonald's existence in the universe at the time. In our corner of the world, Burger Chef ruled!

    However "cool" the physical plant appeared, the "coolest" part was the parking lot, or should we say, cruising the parking lot. This ritual became almost symbolic of "cool."

    Turning our car into the parking lot from Buckhannon Pike, we ascended somewhat steeply, then drove to the right of the restaurant, proceeded around the back and then beyond the other side, finally descending gradually back down to the Pike. Concurrently, we would peer through the glass into the Burger Chef to see if any pretty girls just happened to be there. Of course, if there were, we had to shift to neutral and "rev" the engine for attention. Anyone who was anybody would park their cars along the far fence and just sit there for hours. We would pass by and wave or occasionally stop if inclined or invited to do so. If we passed and waved, it was "mandatory" upon exiting the parking lot onto Buckhannon Pike, to "peel out" (also known as "lay some rubber," or "screech the tires.")

While growing up, everyone experiences a lot of fun firsts. For the Toompas twins, cruising the Burger Chef with our own car was probably the most memorable. It seemed to serve as a right of passage into young adulthood in the Nutter Fort area. We vividly remember driving our Ford Pinto with the windows down, waving to the ever-present Charlie Cutlip, with "Bad Company" blaring appropriately *Movin` On* from our eight-track tape player. We could see the reflection, in the plate glass, of our Pinto and its slotted, deep-dish, mag. wheels when driving around and around "The Chef" multiple times on a Saturday night. Sometimes we would be ahead of, or not too far behind our friend, P.J. Raymond, and his yellow Chevy Vega station wagon, having agreed to rendezvous at the Chef after earlier communications on our CB radios.

We have great memories of hanging out at the Burger Chef, ordering a Big Chef, fries and a Coke or milkshake. What we wouldn't give to just pop the clutch and spin those D-60's of our Ford Pinto just one more time as we go...*Cruising The Burger Chef*.

EGGed On

Due to our skinny physique, our un-coordination, and lack of talents, when the teenage years arrived, we twins had very little self-confidence. Why would we? We were both identically scrawny, homely, even sort of ugly. As the famous comedian George Carlin once said, "People will forgive you if you're ugly, but not if you have the same ugliness walking right beside you!" And, of course, WE did!

Once while with Dad on the back porch of our Lustron metal house, Stanley was feeling down on himself. Most unattractive kids could just stay away from a mirror if they wanted to ignore their appearance and improve their outlook on life. Not us. We saw exactly what we looked like every day, just by being with one another. We served as a constant reminder to each other of our inadequacies. So on this day, Stanley interrupts Dad as he was reading the Clarksburg Telegram and says, "I don't like the way I look, I'm ugly." Dad moved the newspaper, removed his Amphora filled pipe from his mouth, leaned toward Stanley and said, "God loves you and thinks you look fine." Okay, big deal, Stanley thought to himself and then asked, "How do you know that to be true?" Dad confidently pronounced, "Because, honey...HE...made two of you!" He then winked and returned perusing the newspaper.

This was our wonderful father at his best. We twins loved him so much and never wanted to disappoint him. Of course we did, but we really do not think it was very often. Our manners were good. Our grades were good.

Sometimes, when we were very young, we would upset Mom, and she would chase us unsuccessfully with "the paddle." She rarely caught us or spanked us much. Her heart just wasn't in it. However, she would often repeat the overused cliché, "Wait till your Father gets home." Upon arriving home stressed from a 12 hour work day at the drug store, Dad would occasionally over-react, and begin spanking us with authority. At this moment, a mysterious dichotomy ensued. Mom, who had informed him about our transgressions and encouraged him to punish us in the first place, suddenly came to our defense? She would beg Dad to stop paddling us! We could hear her scream, "They are so skinny, you are going to hurt them" and "Edward, you are going to kill them." Sometimes, Mom would begin to cry! One time Mom inserted her hand between the paddle and our backside to try and "protect" us. Her hand was red for days.

After we had recovered from our paddling and stopped crying, Dad would always insist that we both hop up on his lap where he would give us both a BIG hug. He would always explain that this punishment hurt him much worse than it hurt us. As kids, we did not understand that, but of course, as parents, we do now.

Usually when we disappointed Dad, it involved food. Dad consistently and demonstratively insisted we eat all of our food on our plate. Maybe this occurred because we were so embarrassingly underdeveloped compared to the rest of the neighborhood kids, or because Dad, born in 1928 and raised during the depression, just could not tolerate wasting food. First off, breakfast was always wonderful and never a problem. Ditto lunch. It was always the evening meal where confrontation ensued. It usually involved cooked cabbage, cooked broccoli, cooked carrots, cooked spinach, cooked cauliflower, or a rare bean of some sort that was not green. Even though it is now common knowledge that some of these vegetables would be healthier if eaten raw, that was not the prevailing thought in the mid to late 1960s. When Dad demanded that we eat what was on our plate, we astutely responded that we had not put it there in the first place!

Then, taking a page from Grandma Irene's playbook, he would try to embarrass us into eating the food. Dad would say, "Your cousins Bruce and Jeff would eat it, and that is why they are so much bigger than you!" We retorted that we did not care and that we would give this to them if he wished. That did it! We can visualize Dad rising from his chair and instructing us to sit there until we had at least tried it—all evening, if that's what it took!

A couple of times we can remember placing the most infinitesimal amount of the offending substance on our forks and then with great consternation, placing it cautiously in our mouths. It immediately grossed us out and caused a gag reflex. Our Father was incredulous. After experiencing that a couple of times, we simply refused to try it. Dad would leave the table, go into the living room and Mom would start cleaning dishes while we sat at the kitchen table. We "out waited" him. On one occasion, it seemed as though hours passed by. Finally Dad would yell in and tell us to get up and go do something. We twins had persevered. Dad was very disappointed.

Stanley struggled for the longest time to learn to swallow pills. Of course to Dad, being a Pharmacist, this was unacceptable! He instructed, urged, yelled, threatened and still Stanley just stood in the kitchen, his cries echoing off the metal walls, scared to swallow some Vitamin A capsules, lest he choke. With Dad's temper erupting, and with him about to turn Stanley upside down, Stanley "accidentally" swallowed the pill. Dad was again embarrassed concerning all the effort utilized on this simple procedure. This episode and the other food refusal incidents were minor compared to what we are about to reveal.

One Sunday afternoon, nearing the end of our senior year in high school, the phone rang, Dad answered, listened briefly, hung up, shook his head in disgust, then stated, "I can't believe it, but some hooligans were out Saturday night throwing eggs and have made a mess all over the streets of Nutter Fort! I am so glad my sons would never do anything like that." Stephen and Stanley stole an uneasy glance at each other, then Dad said, "You boys were out last night, did you see anything?"

"Nothing to report" was our response. More accurately, nothing we wanted to report. One week later, the truth surfaced and all details were revealed. We had indeed been out. In fact, we were part of the guilty party. It was the worst thing we ever did. In one respect, isn't that fortunate? On the other hand, it was still inappropriate behavior. Our Dad was crestfallen.

"This close to graduation," Dad says, "Top of your class, leaders at school, and you risk your reputations and possibly cause property damage?" We assured him that nothing happened that a little soap and water would not remedy. He continued, "I thought you boys were more mature than that! Soon you will be heading off to college. I can NOT believe this." There may have been eggs splattered all over the streets of Nutter Fort, but as far as Dad was concerned, there was egg "on his face!" It is the greatest of understatements to say that he was disappointed.

We are unsure of how the egg battle began. But needless to say, once initiated by one group, retaliation by the other was inevitable. Neither side wanted to be "beaten" (pun intended.) This was not a rival gang fight, or a feud initiated over someone's "stolen" girlfriend. In fact, all the participants were friends and it began as innocent fun with our "sunny sides up" (can't help ourselves), but ended with us "scrambling" (should have resisted this one) for cover. In the end, the "yolk" (in poor taste, {in and of itself, a pun}) was on us and Dad's repulsion hit the "boiling" (sorry) point. He was fried (we'll stop now!).

We do recall that we traversed just about every neighborhood street that evening. Hiding out, driving with our headlights off, changing vehicles, and using other improvised strategic tactics of community engagement. There must have been 12 or 14 teenagers involved, one of which was our good friend, Bernie Maze.

Bernie was larger than we twins and certainly more unconventional. So, we dubbed him "Big, Bad, Bernie." He loved the nickname. We really were quite good friends during high school and would later, in fact, share an apartment with him as sophomores in college. However on this fateful evening, we ended up on opposing sides, and if not for that, our Father may have never found out about our involvement. Let us explain.

That bizarre Saturday night did result with egg covered neighborhood streets and residents rising on Sunday morning, readying for church, soon to discover egg on their innocently parked cars. In contrast, the participants vehicles were washed that night, after combat, and escaped identification.

In fact, after the battle, we twins washed our Pinto, drove it through Arbutos Park to a street behind our rear neighbor's house, and instituted a plan. We did not want to get egg on our clean car nor did we want our "enemies" to know we had gone home. So, Stanley jumped out, ran through the neighbor's yard, bisected the hedges, traversed our back yard and emerged at our driveway. He quickly started Dad's car, pulled it out of the driveway, and left it idling. He then ran to the garage, manually opened the very heavy garage door, all the while silently counting. On cue, Stephen appeared, running stealth with lights off, and pulled the Pinto into the driveway and on into the garage. Stephen hopped out, shut the garage door and locked it. Stanley, simultaneously, pulled Dad's Dodge into the exact same spot in the driveway where it had been parked all evening, got out, ran to the side of the garage, entered, and locked the side door.

Our plan had been implemented to perfection, but was it successful? We waited and soon found out. Peering through a window, a couple of our rival's automobiles drove slowly along in front of our house. What they saw was: no twins, no Pinto, and the residence appearing exactly as it had appeared the many other times they drove by earlier in the evening, right down to Mr. Toompas' Dodge parked in the driveway. Success! The battles were over. Unbelievably, no witnesses existed and none of the combatants squealed. Even in high school, the next week, the event remained covert.

As every adult realizes, a week in the life of a teenager is a very long period of time, and by that particular week's end, we had sort of forgotten the entire episode. But not Big Bad Bernie! For some reason, he did not take it all in good fun as the rest of us had, and apparently harbored some ill-will. Unbeknownst to us, revenge was on his mind.

Stanley had just finished taking a girl home from a date on the following Saturday night, when "splat," "splat." Out of nowhere and certainly unexpected, two eggs hit his windshield. Stanley was driving Dad's Dodge Monaco and knew this was not good. He drove directly to the car wash, hosed off Dad's luxury car, put the wand away, when suddenly Bernie appeared. Emerging from his blue Mercury Bobcat, he engaged Stanley, holding, of all things, a big bowl of baked beans and peanut butter! With spatula in hand and a big smile on his face, he began bombarding Dad's car with the concoction. He slung the beans everywhere, and covered the windshield, rear-view mirrors and the beautiful metallic green paint of Dad's luxury car. When finished, his posture embodied that of a victor. He then drove away. Stanley had no money left to wash the car. Uh-oh!

So, Stanley had to drive the peanut butter and bean covered car home, hook up the hose, and wash the automobile in the driveway at about 11:30 p.m. Dad, alerted by the sound of running water, exited the house. He was alarmed about his car's appearance and began asking for an explanation. We twins reluctantly informed him of all that had transpired that night and the previous weekend. Stephen helped clean the car and it was a good thing; those baked beans seemed to have been glued onto the finish because of the peanut butter!

We twins had won the battle but ultimately lost the war to Bernie, but that was not the worst result. More so, we had disappointed our Father.

Never again were we to be...*EGGed On*.

Second Chance in the Second City

Truth be known, Stanley hated attending college at WVU (West Virginia University). He went from BMOC (Big Man on Campus), at least in his own mind, at high school, to total anonymity at this large state college. Stanley had many personal items stolen and got trapped once on the PRT (Personal Rapid Transit) at the midpoint of the elevated rail! After waiting over an hour to be "rescued," he had to walk back to the dorm on the PRT tracks, in the rain! His academics suffered the first semester with a GPA below 3.0 with 19 credit hours. He even dropped a class in his major during the first semester of his sophomore year! Without a clear direction, Stanley struggled during his first three semesters of college. In stark contrast, twin brother Stephen flourished his first 2 years of college, maintaining a near 4.0 GPA. Committed to a future in Pharmacy, Stephen sailed through his academic endeavors and straight into Pharmacy school.

Disappointed with Stanley's achievements compared to identical twin Stephen, Dad sent Stanley to the Eye Doctor to determine whether his vision system could be at fault. After the appointment, Stanley's vision system was deemed to be consistent, but his vision for the future was MUCH clearer. He decided to attempt to become an Optometrist.

Knowing he had almost no margin of error remaining, Stanley improved his academics dramatically. Classes became easier to focus (pun intended) on, now that there was a clear (Eye Doctors love these!) goal in sight (we should stop now, but probably will not.) By the first semester of his junior year, Stanley was applying to Optometry schools. Granted two interviews, the one in Philadelphia did not go well, but the one in Chicago nearly did not "Go" at all!

Stephen was too engrossed with Pharmacy school to take time to accompany Stanley to Chicago for the interview, so our roommate, Mike Alastanos, graciously volunteered to ride along. Mike, an accounting major, also hailed from Clarksburg, but had attended our rival High School, Washington-Irving. We twins had known "of him" in high school only. That all changed at the end of our freshman year at college in 1977.

While sitting in the basement of our freshman dormitory with our old friend, Bernie Maze, we were discussing living arrangements for our Sophomore year but needed one more roommate for the considered apartment. To our left we heard someone coming, and turned to see Mike walking toward us. Exchanging pleasantries as was our custom, Mike asked what we were doing. We told him we were looking for a roommate. He immediately responded, "You've got to be kidding, I'm looking for a place to stay next year!" Within minutes, his dilemma and ours was solved. We became roommates and a lifelong friendship commenced. Mike is now an accountant in Clarksburg and his wife, Becky, also an accountant, is employed by Stephen's Drug Store, Town and Country. Mike is of full-blooded Greek descent and his nickname is, "Greek."

Stanley takes the story solo from here:

Neither Mike nor I had ever been west of central Ohio, so we were both excited about the excursion to the Midwest. Driving the twin's brown, 1978, Toyota Corolla station wagon (nicknamed Kimota), we set out for Chicago and my upcoming Optometry School interview. It was a very cold and typically blustery night when we arrived at the "Windy City" in late March, 1979.

Remember, GPS technology did not exist, so we relied on my Rand-McNally Road Atlas. On a map, the colored lines representing roads in Chicago do not appear all that dissimilar to the ones in West Virginia. As you can well imagine, we were two quite naive 20 year olds driving into, what at that time was, the second largest American city. With Mike driving, we hit the Dan Ryan expressway after nightfall. It was our plan to drive by the Optometry school before heading off to our hotel.

The 8-lane Dan Ryan expressway was much more intimidating than two small-town West Virginia boys could have ever imagined. Without too much of a problem however, we found the appropriate exit, and began searching for South Michigan Avenue when the unexpected occurred. We both inadvertently ignored a stoplight on Martin Luther King Jr. Drive, and subsequently did not see it turning red. This scenario was not totally incomprehensible, since the stoplights back in West Virginia were all hanging directly over the intersections, and these were positioned to the side of the street.

Bang! Halfway through the intersection a car collides with us. It hit us directly in the back passenger side door. At impact, Mike instinctively extended his right arm across my chest. The car spins around and comes to a stop. We were not wearing seat-belts, yet fortunately our heads did not hit the windshield. When I exited the car, I dropped to my knees for a few seconds trying to recover from the initial shock of the situation. Mike was shaken up and worried about my well-being. The driver of the car which hit us was not injured, but continually complained about the damage to his vehicle. I tried to assure him that my insurance would cover the damages, but he was not convinced due to our out-of-state license. Though late at night, local citizens quickly began gathering along the sidewalks, observing the crash scene.

The police arrived in an amazingly short period of time, which relieved both of us. They began asking questions and as one officer was looking at the license plate, the other asked Mike, "Where are you from?" Mike answered, "West Virginia." The officer grinned and said, "Welcome to Chicago."

Of course the accident was our fault, but fortunately, though the car was significantly damaged, it was still drivable. The Chicago police realized that we West Virginia boys were like "fish out of water" here on the south-side of Chicago, so they graciously suggested an escort, lest we end up in Lake Michigan. Free at last (well, we were on Martin Luther King Jr. Drive), unharmed but still shaken, we followed them down and over one block, drove by the Illinois College of Optometry (ICO), then preceded to the Chicago downtown Holiday Inn on Madison Street. We thanked them for their kindness, checked into our hotel, occupied our room, counted our blessings, and immediately called our families.

Upon calling home, my parents were understandably upset, yet relieved that we were not injured. I am quite sure Mike conveyed the same message to his parents that I had to mine, but I cannot absolutely verify this, as his conversation was entirely in Greek! Yes, Mike is fluent in the Greek language. Mike felt compelled to not only talk to his parents but also to my Dad (in English), and told him that he had "goofed up!" Dad told him not to worry about it. He was just happy we were okay. We thanked God that we were alive, uninjured, and indeed had a second chance at a normal life. When the adrenaline rush wore off, we both finally fell asleep.

The next morning, with no further incidents, we made our way over to 3241 S. Michigan Ave. and arrived at ICO for my interview. There was actually one positive that emerged from the car accident; I was very loose and more relaxed than I would have normally been, so, the interview went well. So well in fact, that the interviewer, Dr. Sunny Sanders, actually stated, "I have never met anybody quite like you!" I considered this remark a compliment and explained that I was an identical twin, so indeed there was another just like me. She was flabbergasted. I had made a positive impression upon her and hoped it was enough to convince the admissions committee of my worthiness.

On the way home, Mike and I reflected on life, family, religion, purpose etc. I was thankful that the stranger's car did not hit us with a greater impact and further forward, or else I may have been killed and/or significantly injured. Mike continually apologized for the car's damage, but considering what could have happened, it was really no big deal. This shared experience impacted (terrible pun) and cemented our relationship. Friends forever.

In late April of 1979, A few weeks after arriving home from the Windy City, I received a letter in the mail from ICO. Due to the significant competition for admission, I was prepared for whatever news the letter might hold. I opened it with my roommates Greek, Mike George, and brother Stephen surrounding me. Incredibly, I was accepted. Competition for admission had been intense. Most applicants had a four year degree. I was completing my third year. Many had near 4.0 GPA's. I finished WVU with a 3.5. I had improved greatly since beginning at WVU, but my record paled in comparison to many future ICO classmates.

No doubt, the interview put me over the top. A year or so later, the interviewer, Dr. Sanders, verified my assumption and revealed that she had ardently "went to bat" for me and pleaded with the admissions committee to accept me. She explained to the committee that I was one of the most unique interviews she had ever conducted and that she would guarantee that I would make a fine Optometrist. She later revealed that I was one of the final students chosen for admission.

During my first year of Professional School, Dr. Sanders encouraged me to excel so as not to make her "look bad" considering the great effort she had made considering admission on my behalf. I am proud to announce that I subsequently made her proud, as I completed my Doctorate degree in 1983, Cum Laude, in the top 27 of 147 graduates. I have practiced Optometry for 28+ years and have enjoyed it immensely.

I owe thanks to Dr. Sunny Sanders and that impressive 1979 interview for my ultimate admission to Illinois College of Optometry. I owe thanks to "Greek" for accompanying me to Chicago, and we owe thanks to God for allowing both of us a...*Second Chance in the Second City*.

The "Non-Campaign," Campaign

You already know that Stanley did get accepted to Optometry School. But at the beginning of the second semester of his junior year at WVU in 1979, the reality was that his chances, like his physique, were very slim. He would probably have to stay at WVU for one more year, excel academically and re-apply for admission. Again, he did not embrace the uninviting large university and did not relish the likelihood of another year of undergraduate studies. If however, that was to be his fate, he pondered on how to make his life at WVU more palatable. Stanley continued to miss the good old days of high school student council, so, he went "back to the future" and decided to run for one of eleven Student Government Board of Directors positions. He filed in January of 1979, announced his candidacy, and the race was on.

WVU engulfed most of Morgantown and had two major campuses connected by the aforementioned futuristic PRT. We twins lived on the Evansdale campus. Stephen was within walking distance of all of his pharmacy school classes at the Med Center. He was encouraging and guaranteed Stanley that he could influence some Pharmacy school students to vote for his twin brother. Our cousin, Jeff, lived on the downtown campus. Running in different circles than us, and with a non-medical major, he could easily influence a different group of voters.

One of our roommates, Mike George, now a Dentist in Uniontown PA., was also very supportive of Stanley's run for office. Our other roommate, Mike Alastanos, volunteered to serve as Stanley's campaign manager. (By the way, this all took place before the car crash mentioned in the previous story "Second Chance in the Second City.") After all, we reasoned, with two "real" Greek names like Alastanos and Toompas, maybe we could capture some of the "Greek" (fraternity) vote? Seemed logical at the time.

Stanley takes the story solo from here:

We decided immediately to make this a low-key campaign, or what was ultimately dubbed the "non-campaign," campaign. I spent a total of $6.30 (Yes, the decimal point is in the correct position, if the editor and printer stayed true to my original manuscript; only six dollars and 30 cents!), which allowed for the making of a few signs, which we placed in conspicuous places around campus. That's it for expenditures! I decided I was going to win this election with my message, not money, with my personality, not paraphernalia or propaganda. So, I attended all of the candidate forums, which in retrospect were disappointing, as there were usually more candidates on stage than prospective student voters in the audience! Nonetheless, the forums allowed me to be discovered by the Associate Editor of the newspaper, *The Daily Antheneum*. Her name was Kathe Knotts. She liked me and my unique, fresh, and entertaining approach to the election. She also appreciated my low budget style and my "outsider" status. Though a dark-horse candidate, she considered me as the alternative to the status quo, and passionately endorsed my candidacy in person, even if unable to do so officially, in print.

Twenty-five students ran for eleven spots. Hard to believe, but some of these students spent literally hundreds and hundreds of dollars on their campaigns. These were significant amounts of money in 1979! Apparently, a resume-building win was worth the expense, if it meant eventually getting accepted to Law School! Some candidates were backed by Fraternity or Sorority houses. Mike and I felt like we were in a very large lake, in a very small canoe, surrounded by yachts! However, we persevered. Nervous as election day approached, we knew my chances for election were improbable, yet not nearly as impossible as it appeared when the campaign began. Unorthodox to the end, and no longer unknown, I had a chance.

In February of 1979, in Morgantown, West Virginia, election day came and went. Vote counting continued into the night. After much pacing and anxiety, the phone rang. It was Kathe, the official results had been delivered to the Daily Antheneum...I WON! I had finished tenth of eleven chosen, but I had won. What a thrill and an enjoyable process this election had been. Maybe WVU wasn't so bad after all!

To make a long story short, I served on the Board of Directors for only a very short time. Two months after the surprising election, the mail arrived with my unexpected acceptance letter to Optometry School. I had to make a choice and subsequently resigned the Board of Directors position. What a shame, I had just begun to enjoy undergrad school and I really embraced student government. By the way, I served with Student Body President Craig Underwood, son to the famous two term, albeit, 40 years apart, Governor of West Virginia, Cecil Underwood.

My unique campaign and subsequent victory garnered a lot of attention. A Morgantown journalist wrote an article about it and distributed it to some state newspapers. The article, "Toompas Successful in Stretching the Dollar," was flattering and highly complimentary. Also, a very detailed article with photograph appeared in the Daily Antheneum the following September chronicling the previous campaign, my resignation, and Optometry aspirations.

In retrospect, I am glad I left WVU to attend Optometry School, but regret missing the opportunity to have served in student government for an entire academic year. Though some bad memories remain from my undergraduate experience at WVU, they are overshadowed by the positive results of...*The "Non-Campaign," Campaign.*

I'm The One The Other Isn't—Book Two

Tuesday, February 13, 1979

final tally

(note: official election winners typed in bold)

PRESIDENT/vice-pres.

Craig Underwood / **Gayle Armstrong**	**1832**
Mark Williams / Bob Burkhardt	1392
John Albano / John Giannuzzi	1337

BOARD OF DIRECTORS

Joe Carr	**1870**
Sharon Rapp	**1687**
Biff Clark	**1544**
Paul Templeton	**1453**
Nick Plesich	**1443**
Lorrie Brouse	**1363**
Tyler Bullock	**1317**
Jack Wilson	**1133**
John Rice	**1091**
Stanley Toompas	**1029**
Rich Kolosky	1017
Yvonne Miller	1009
Brian Winkesdorffer	959
Clare Shockley	939
Doug Richardson	896
Mike Benninger	826
Mark Sorsain	772
Mark Rogers	763
Evelyn Tomaszewski	758
Doug Baldey	732
Keith Carnahan	644
Fred Staker	638
Theodore Gierlich	367
Hilde Edler	347
Andrew Gamber	335

ATHLETIC COUNCIL

Barry Zimmerman	**943**
Ben Francavilla	**940**
Kathy Klausing	**866**
Charlie Brown	**824**
Dave Hanna	549
Doug Salvati	508
Kevin Mason	471
Bill Huff	441
Robert Waggoner	404
Milton Richards	347
Dicky Gunnoe	339
Brad Russell	316
Dick Myers	245

Toompas Successful In Stretching The Dollar

MORGANTOWN — With the current rate of inflation, a dollar doesn't go very far but Stan Toompas, a graduate of Roosevelt-Wilson High, proved that six dollars and thirty cents can go a long, long way.

Toompas was recently elected to a seat on the West Virginia University Student Administration Board of Directors. Unlike the other students who were elected he didn't spend $200, $100 or even $50. He spent only $6.30.

Armed only with a set of felt-tipped markers, some paper, and an endearing sense of humor, Toompas set out to win the votes of his fellow students.

Amidst a volley of speeches and campaign promises from the other 23 students running for office, the young Clarksburg resident maintained one goal, "I do not have thousands of handbills, buttons, stickers or pencils, just a few posters. I hope to win on personality, not paraphenalia or propoganda."

What young Toompas lacked in campaign funds he more than made up for in personality. Tears of laughter streamed down the faces of the audience as Stan started his speeches. "I don't believe in fancy slogans like 'Vote Joe Apple and get to the core of the problem,' or 'Vote Speedy Racer. It's my way or the highway.''

On a more serious note, he would go on to explain that he had one commitment, and that was to the students. In closing, he would offer a note of thanks to his campaign manager, Mike Alastanos, who is also a Clarksburg native.

Stan Toompas learned how to stretch a dollar. With only six dollars and thirty cents he set out to win a seat on the Board of Directors, and in the process ended up winning the hearts of an entire University.

Double Dose

From birth though grade school, we were almost impossible to tell apart. As we have mentioned in our first book, we believe our own Mother was confused much of the time. The many times Stevie and Stanley were together, which was almost always, adults would maintain a confused look on their face when encountering us. Eventually they just communicated as if we were a collective, as if we were not just one individual. We are sure that all identical twins can relate to this.

We believe it should not have been THAT difficult considering Stevie's forehead scar caused by an ironing board accident (Reference "Scar" from our first book.) If people could just remember, even for only a short while, that Steve had the scar. But, no adult seemed to make that effort. We twins have concluded that most adults were just too confused and embarrassed when they came in close proximity to us.

As youth, we loved visitors, especially daily ones such as the newspaper delivery boy, the milk man, and the mail man. We would wait for their arrival and we would greet them on the front porch. These same individuals were consistently employed for years, yet none of them could ever tell us apart.

Television burst onto the American landscape in the 1950's. Our first recollection of a TV image was on the black and white TV in 1963. We twins were five years old. In our mind's eye, we can still see the horse drawn, flag-draped casket of President Kennedy, during the funeral processional.

Color television was a giant leap for us and all of mankind (Forgive us for channeling the national pride felt when recalling the grainy images of the first moon landing in 1969.) It was wonderful, with numerous buttons and sliding knobs. So, the way we viewed images on the TV changed, but one thing remained constant; the need for TV repair and maintenance.

Our TV repairman's name was Jack Smith (this is actually his real name), and he visited frequently. Mom just had to have an adequate functioning TV so she would not miss her favorite, "The Mike Douglas Show." Jack spent many hours behind our TV. He would push it away from our living room's front window and remove the back panel. A most patient person, this kind man allowed Stevie and Stanley to watch, talk, and ask questions. We twins were amazed by the complexities encountered, the many colored wires, the multiple vacuum tubes in early models, and the transistors later on. We got to know Jack real well, but he to, could never tell us apart.

Through the years, we believe nurture has trumped nature. At over a half century in age, we both believe we look somewhat different now and should be easily distinguishable when standing beside one another. But when separated, people still have problems knowing which one is which. Let us give you an example of mistaken identities that is typical of that which occurs.

About a dozen years or so ago, when we were 41, Stanley just happened to be in Nutter Fort and decided to stop at Town and Country Drug Store to see Stephen. After visiting with Stephen for a short time, Stanley left. Immediately upon exiting the store, out in the parking lot, a slightly older gentleman approaches Stanley and says, "Hey Stephen, why aren't you working? Is it your quitting time already?" Stanley, not wanting to offend and having experienced similar situations such as this, quickly responds, "Sir, I know you think I am Stephen, but I am not. I am actually his identical twin brother Stanley."

A very puzzled look came upon this man's face, as he allowed himself a moment to absorb "Stephen's(?)" statement. The man then leaned back ever so slightly and tilted his head in a questioning manner. Convinced of Stephen's attempts at humor, he then confidently announced, "GOOD ONE, STEVE," as he punched Stanley firmly in the right arm! Shaking his head he entered the drug store laughing. Stanley got in his car and drove off, accurately visualizing what was about to transpire.

The gentleman walked through the drug store, back to the Pharmacy counter and looked up and was immediately flabbergasted! There in the pharmacy, working, was Stephen. The man's face became blood red with embarrassment as he instantly realized he had just hit a total stranger! Stammering and stuttering, explaining to Stephen what had just occurred, and repeatedly apologizing for his actions, he remained visibly distraught for quite some time. While filling prescriptions, Stephen and his assistants continually reassured their customer that this type of mistaken identity incidents occurred often, and everything was just fine. In fact, Stanley wouldn't give it a second thought, even if he did have a bruise developing on his arm as he drove back to Philippi.

Stephen eventually handed this embarrassed customer his single prescription medicine. But on this day in Stephen's pharmacy, as it concerned the Toompas twins, this man was subject to a...*Double Dose*.

Double Vision

We both assumed that, as we proceeded through college developing our own individuality and separate niches, identity confusion would dissipate. Boy did we miss the mark on that one. Read on and see just how wrong we were.

During our third year at WVU, Stephen was in his first year of Pharmacy School, while Stanley was continuing to major in Biology. Hoping for a career in Optometry, Stanley applied to three Optometry schools. Two schools granted interviews, Illinois College of Optometry(ICO) in Chicago (Reference story "Second Chance in The Second City") and Pennsylvania College of Optometry (PCO) in Philadelphia.

Dad drove Stanley to Philadelphia in early February of 1979 for his interview at PCO. Typically difficult winter weather conditions existed, yet they seemed to have no problem passing over the West Virginia hills in Dad's 1976, rear-wheel drive, metallic silver and maroon Dodge Aspen. Today, we fret if our children do not have front wheel drive or all-wheel drive vehicles, but we digress as is customary.

When arriving in Philadelphia, Dad and Stanley ate a nice dinner, shared a hotel room, rose early the next morning, and drove to campus for the interview. The "City of Brotherly Love" moniker seemed appropriate, but that was just about to change.

Stanley, nervous as always, got called in for his interview. We are unable to recall specifics, but suffice it to say that the interview did not go well. The line of questioning seemed rather odd and quite frankly, nothing like Stanley had expected. Stanley knew the interviewer was not impressed by his responses, yet at the same time, the man seemed distracted. For some reason, Dad was allowed to join the process after a few unproductive minutes.

Eventually, the confused interviewer bluntly asked, "Just why do you want to quit Pharmacy School midstream and begin Optometry school?" Stanley looked at Dad with a "knowing" disappointment. Stanley explains to the interviewer that he is not in Pharmacy school. The gentleman then tilts his folder forward to reveal WVU transcripts that show otherwise. Stanley glances at them and points out that those are NOT his transcripts, but those of his identical twin brother Stephen! WVU had sent the wrong transcripts!

The gentleman indicated that the interview was basically over, as nothing could be learned without the proper transcripts. He did ask a couple of cursory questions out of courtesy to our Father, having made the long arduous trip over the mountains from north-central West Virginia. However, the interviewer considered this entire process a waste of his time, and of course, that did not bode well for Stanley. For the younger generation reading this story—No, we could not fix the situation with a fax! No fax fix (wasn't that fun?) option existed yet. Stanley left Philadelphia dejected. Pennsylvania College of Optometry could not see its way clearly (pun intended) to accept Stanley for admission after this fiasco.

As you know, Stanley did, however, get accepted to Illinois College of Optometry in Chicago and attended there while Stephen was finishing Pharmacy School in Morgantown. We were each on our own, separate, for four years. For example, a few of Stanley's contemporaries in Chicago knew that he had an identical twin, but rarely saw him. The entire identity confusion scenarios stopped abruptly and to be honest, almost forgotten about after we each established our own professional school identities 555 miles apart.

A few years passed. After graduating, Stephen began practicing pharmacology in Nutter Fort, WV, in 1981. Stanley moved to Philippi, WV, and began practicing optometry in 1983. We lived 30 miles apart and worked in two different professional worlds, yet the opportunity for mistaken identities just re-emerged and increased dramatically. We were unprepared as you will see by the following story. It is typical of the identity confusion situations we still face today.

One afternoon, Stanley was in Philippi, when an established patient returned for her annual eye exam. Stanley's senior by forty or so years, they had established a friendly, cordial Doctor-Patient relationship over time. However, on this particular day, things felt awkward. The typical ambiance was absent. There was an obvious tension in her manner and voice. Her conversation was measured. Before beginning the actual vision testing, Stanley garnered enough courage to ask her if something was wrong.

Immediately this refined lady slid forward in the exam chair, leaned toward Stanley and with an accusatory tone replies, "Well yes, quite frankly, there is. I thought you were a committed Christian. What a façade you put on. You are not who you say you are!" Stanley was taken aback. Confused, Stanley asked her how she had arrived at this conclusion. The distinguished lady responded, "I was at the Bridgeport mall this past weekend, and THAT was NOT your wife I saw you with, walking side by side and holding hands!"

Stanley had not been at the mall during the past weekend and was momentarily discombobulated until it suddenly dawned on him; Stephen had been at the mall with his wife. Instantaneously, Stanley realized he had a proper explanation for this awkward allegation, yet could not callously "blurt it out" due to the damaging effects it may have on his concerned patient.

Using his best "bed-side" manner, Stanley denies his presence at the mall and explains it was his identical twin brother, Stephen, that she saw. Leaning back to grasp the meaning of what was just said, the patient gazed at Stanley, realized the veracity of his statement and was visibly shaken and embarrassed by her previous accusations. She was simultaneously devastated, yet relieved, if indeed those conflicting emotions are at once compatible.

Stanley consoled her and explained that this situation of mistaken identity was certainly understandable since we were identical twins. This line of reasoning did not seem to be improving her stricken state. Finally, Stanley leans toward her and calmly reassures her that as a Christian, he was glad she held him accountable. Only someone that truly cared about him and his wife would risk ending the friendship and a professional relationship.

After a few minutes, the patient gathered herself and the eye exam was concluded. The examination revealed this patient's vision was 20/20, but for a transient moment, she complained of...*Double Vision*.

{Special note: Identity confusion issues have become very commonplace over the years. The patient/customer of one twin would see him out somewhere, yet he seemed distant, unfriendly, even rude! Why? Because, it was not him! It was his brother! So, a few years ago we both agreed, that if a stranger approached one of us and acted as if they "knew" us, we would instantly inform them of our "twinness." Also, our patients/customers have said, "I met your brother the other day. I thought it was you, but after I approached him, I found out you were an identical twin!"}

I'm The One The Other Isn't-Book Two

Double Trouble

The previous two stories have revealed that being double can produce trouble. Now we will share with you the flip side; how we can produce trouble, by being double.

One such time was a Philippi Lions Club meeting in the mid to late 1980's, where Stanley, a member, was to present a program on "Eye Care" one evening. Unbeknownst to the general Lions Club membership, Stanley informed Stephen of the meeting time and place and concocted a scheme.

The meeting was held on Alderson-Broaddus College campus in a room adjacent to the kitchen. Stanley "snuck" Stephen into the kitchen area undetected by all but a co-conspiring kitchen staff employee. We purposely dressed in identically matching outfits (the first time in two decades) and possessed identical note cards. Stephen waited by the kitchen door as Stanley sat in the front row seat at the meeting.

The Philippi Lions Club followed the traditional sequence of opening a meeting. Soon the program director stepped forth and introduced the program and the guest speaker for the evening, Dr. Stanley E. Toompas, Optometrist. After a courtesy applause, Stanley began with remarks of a general nature, then paused abruptly to say that he had forgotten something in the kitchen. He excused himself, walked to his left and exited through the kitchen door. Stephen, anxiously awaiting on the other side, took Stanley's glasses (our prescriptions were similar enough to suffice for this purpose of brief deception) placed them on his head and strolled out though the door.

Immediately, Stephen (who all in attendance, "knew" was Stanley), apologized for the delay, and continued the presentation right where Stanley left off, as designated on the prepared index cards! After a brief time, Stephen excused himself for a similar reason to the first, and Stanley came back in the room.

This "switch-a-roo" occurred at least four times, and both of us enjoyed it immensely. Finally, while Stephen was speaking, he told the crowd that he was not feeling well all of a sudden, and that he needed to call his assistant on for some help, and pointed to his left toward the kitchen; in walks Stanley. We, identically dressed, identical twins stood beside one another, in front of a stunned audience. After a brief delay for reality to set in, everyone in attendance began laughing hysterically.

It was fun for everyone that evening at the Philippi Lions Club, and in fact, it may have been the most fun we had had since childhood!

One other occasion of identity deception is worth mentioning. As revealed in our story, "Double, But No Trouble," our identical appearances easily fooled our elementary school teachers when we switched seats. Though in our early 30's, after the Philippi Lion's Club stunt, Stephen wondered if we could still fool a group of people if we were in the same room together.

This time, Stephen concocted the scheme. Though a retail pharmacist at Town and Country Drug Store, for a few years he was also employed by Fairmont State College. He taught Pharmacology to their nursing students. (For the record, Stanley believes that Stephen was an excellent instructor and may have missed his true calling, but we digress.)

One week, faculty member Stephen announced to his students that his twin brother Stanley, an Optometrist, would be a special guest when the class next met, since the topic would be ophthalmic drugs. So, when class time arrived the following week, Stephen entered and sat in a chair in the last row, as if he were the guest. He tilted his head down, busying himself as though reading some notes. Stanley confidently entered the classroom, acting like a teacher, and greeted all of the students in Stephen's customary manner. Confidently striding to the podium in front of the classroom, Stanley summarized last week's topic and announced that this week's topic was eyes and ophthalmic pharmaceuticals.

At this point, the class has absolutely no clue that this is not Stephen teaching the class. Continuing the façade, Stanley announces that he has a guest joining the class today, points toward the back of the classroom, and introduces his twin brother, . Stanley(?), to the class! The entire class turns, Stephen gives a cursory wave. Stanley introduces him as an Optometrist who is here to assist with Ophthalmic drug questions. We play it straight as an arrow. No revealing grins or smirks. Without a sliver of suspicion, the unsuspecting class re-positions itself to face forward.

Stanley, the long-suffering actor with the more difficult role playing the part of instructor Stephen, nonetheless plays the part perfectly. He announces the proper page number to turn to in their books, and stoically continues. Still, no student doubts that Stephen is not teaching the class. Remember, Stanley was very convincing, as he is a master of the subject material, since it is OCULAR Pharmacology!

After a few sentences, Stanley, as Stephen, asks Stephen, as Stanley, a question. Stephen stands, answers the question, walks forward, and joins Stanley at the podium. Juxtaposed, a few students become aware of the deception. Soon after, we reveal our true identities! Truth be known, there were still a few students that were totally confused and a more detailed explanation ensued. Everyone in attendance enjoyed the charade.

After the laughing ceased, Stephen the Pharmacist, began instructing the class about the eye and ocular pharmacology, deferring to guest expert Stanley, the Optometrist, on matters of practical concern.

In the end, Stephen's scheme was successful. On this night, these college students learned about and personally experienced...*Double Trouble.*

Silver Celebration

    The summer of 1979 seemed typical enough and in some respects better than the previous two college breaks. Stephen was full of self-confidence having achieved Deans List the first two semesters in Pharmacy school. Stanley was finished with WVU and readying himself to go to Chicago for Optometry School. As all elder readers of this text understand, "time" is forever as a young man, so we knew that we had the ENTIRE summer before facing our separation day (references story by the same name.) It was an eventful, activity laden summer.
    Our cousin Jeff got married on June 30 of 1979. Stanley wore a blue suit and Stephen wore a green suit to the wedding, both purchased at Melet's in uptown Clarksburg. The wedding was held in downtown Morgantown with the reception in Star City. We mean no disrespect, but the highlight of the summer for us was not our closest cousin's wedding, it was a wedding anniversary! To be exact, it was our Parents 25th Wedding Anniversary on June 13 and wow,

did we have a party. But before we tell you about that, a little review is in order.

After we twins had completed our first year of college in the summer of 1977, our parents finally decided to move out of THE metal house. The Lustron home that dominates our childhood memories, with all of its unconventionalities. The one written about in our first book with the very cold tile covered concrete floors in the bedrooms and the static producing carpet combined with the resultant electric shock when touching the metal walls in the living and dining room areas. Like an oven in the summer with no air conditioning, and an ice box in the winter with no fireplace and inadequate ceiling radiated heat, Mom and Dad after 19 years, wanted a "real" house. They were not quite as sentimental as we twins were when the front door was shut for the last time. We had gone back to WVU for the '77 fall semester; 115 Mandan Road was now a memory.

Truth be known, when we were in middle school, our parent's considered building a house near our Uncle, Don Hutson. When that fell through, they came within a whisker of purchasing a house in Bridgeport between our Sophomore and Junior year in high school. Even though it was a beautiful "real" house, we twins protested loudly, as we did not want to change high schools and leave our friends. Dad actually listened and decided it was more important for us to have consistency in education versus living in a new house, and so he postponed any possible move.

"Shocking" as the old house was, it was even more shocking for we twins to finally live in a "normal" home. The house number was much the same at 1105 (what's a zero after all?), but that was the only similarity! It had an attached, two stall garage! It had a basement like all of our childhood friend's homes. The house even had an upstairs and an attic. It was over three times larger than the old metal house! Each twin finally had a bedroom to call their own. So, at our college apartment, we shared a bedroom, but on weekends we came home to our own rooms! What a unique and initially unexpectedly unsettling experience that was.

We actually had wallpaper on our bedroom walls! That is another bit of "common sense" that we twins lacked as youth; we had no idea what wallpaper was! Well, we did now, and it was beautiful. No more drab gray-enameled, vertical-paneled metal walls. We each hung pictures on our walls! Real framed photographs, plaques, etc. What a joy this simple action engendered. We twins were just amazed that the new home had 2 ½ bathrooms! What a luxury. The entire family was accustomed to sharing just one for 19 years.

As previously stated, the old metal house did not have a fireplace. This house did not have "a" fireplace either ……….. it had "TWO" fireplaces! Upon seeing this for the first time, Stephen and Stanley both wondered which was more difficult for Santa; using the front door at the metal house, or deciding which chimney to use at this place? Maybe if we had grown up here, Santa would have descended one chimney for Stanley, and the other for Stephen.

The new home had a downstairs also, which included a knotty-pine lined den, with room enough for a pool table. The new kitchen was bigger than our old kitchen and dining room combined! Over in the corner was our own, personal, Maytag washer and dryer. (By the way, the Maytags are still working perfectly 35 years later!) For the first time ever, Mom could do her laundry at home! She was 47 years old. You probably can imagine just how excited Mom was about this development. No more trips to the laundry mat. No more piles of dirty clothes. She could wash as needed, conveniently at home. She was absolutely thrilled. We twins could only wonder what we would have done, if we had grown up here, with all the extra time not spent at the laundry mat. The new house was huge and it was absolutely nothing like the old metal house, it actually had "real" shingles on a conventional roof! The 2-stall, attached garage had a workbench that Uncle Bud built as a housewarming gift.

We twins began feeling more "normal" after moving there. The best part? No more static electricity shocks! Very few of our old high school friends ever saw the new house. One exception was one of our best childhood friends, Lisa Boomer. She not only saw it, she helped to clean it before we moved in. We believe she volunteered because she was just so happy that we abnormal twins were now able to live in a normal house.

Our metal home had so little space (less than 1,000 square feet) and no room for entertainment of guests. That all changed with the new house in 1977, and by the summer of 1979, it was time to have a "real" party!

As of this writing, both Stephen and his Kim, and Stanley and his Kim, have been married 30 years. We had no huge celebrations for our 25th, let alone our 30th wedding anniversaries. Mom and Dad's 25th was different. Encouraged by our cousin Leslie, who informed we clueless twins that our parent's 25th wedding anniversary was approaching, we immediately and expediently organized a wonderful surprise party.

After much deliberation, the final plan was agreed upon and subsequently followed to perfection. Mom and Dad accompanied Uncle Bud and Aunt Dot to dinner that evening. Upon leaving the house, our parents asked us what our plans were for the evening. Stanley said he was getting together with his girlfriend Kim, (which was NOT a lie), and Stephen said that he had no specific plans for himself (also NOT a lie.) As soon as they departed, we sprung into action.

All of the invited guests were to begin arriving at about one half hour after our parents departed and all were to be in the house about one half hour before our folks arrived home. A window of 2 hours existed and it could not have worked more perfectly. Leslie arrived first and handled the entire food situation, which included, fruit trays, vegetable platters, cheese trays, chips with dip, etc. As guests arrived, Stephen led them to Stanley at the front door, who welcomed them in and explained the evening's scheme. Stephen then took their car keys and drove their cars to a pre-arranged neighbor's driveway. We enlisted multiple neighbors in our plot so that a multitude of cars would go unnoticed by our parents. Remember, this alone was quite an achievement, as these were all "new" neighbors less then 2 years prior.

About five minutes before the designated time of their return, we had all the guests seated and the lights out. Uncle Bud pulled into the driveway exactly when expected. We know the reader may think that this accomplishment is no big deal, but we beg to differ. Remember, we had no cell phones, so actually it still amazes us to this day that the timing was so perfect. Our parents entered the front door into the dark foyer and took two steps into the living room to turn on a light and ... "Surprise!"

Close relatives and friends from throughout their married life were in attendance. Among the guests were Mr. Moore, the pharmacist at Bland's when Dad began in 1954, after Dad was discharged from his Korean War service. Also attending was Mr. Jim Caravasos, a pharmacy classmate of Dad's. Our old neighbors from Mandan Road, Smitty and Nell were in attendance as well as Mom's best friends, Rose and Rae Goodwin.

As the night progressed, we began to realize what a magical evening this had been. Many guests brought gifts and we have never seen our Mom and Dad have so much fun...together. The photographs we took are priceless and the obvious joy experienced by our parents was worth all the effort. We thanked Uncle Bud and Aunt Dot for aiding the cause and timing the return perfectly. We thanked all the neighbors who permitted the use of their driveways. Most of all we thanked cousin Leslie. Without her awareness, initiative, and efforts there would certainly have been no party.

Fast forward; Dad died shortly after our parent's 40th wedding anniversary in August of 1994. Many friends who had attended that party in 1979 have also passed on. During those 15 years, Dad repeatedly stated that he had enjoyed the gathering immensely and was proud of the fact that he had a "real" home to accommodate the gathering for their...*Silver Celebration*.

Separation Day

Stevie and Stanley were inseparable as young children. We were twins, Xerox copies, identical in every way. We were linked emotionally and spiritually. We had our own unique communication system. We had the same likes and dislikes, and we shared everything. We were born together and were meant to stay together. However, the administration and teachers at grade school attempted to separate us at the beginning of first grade. They were unsuccessful. What nature brought forth together, no one should have attempted to separate. Our unyielding wills endured and we attended grade school...together!

The authorities had greater success when we entered junior high school in 7th grade. It was a small junior high with two separate homerooms and two classes for each subject (besides gym.) We are unsure why they felt this action was necessary, as the classes were taught by the same teachers and were exactly alike. We twins still studied together and helped one another at home, and shared the same locker at school. We still walked to and from school together and early on, wore identical outfits!

In high school, we had many separate classes, yet attended classes together for those subjects only taught for one class period such as Latin 2, Physics, and Trigonometry/Calculus. We studied together, walked or drove to school together, shared a car, shared clothes, and shared the same small room at the metal house throughout high school.

After high school graduation, we went off to college at WVU …….. together. Even though Stanley had applied and was accepted to West Virginia Wesleyan, when reality set in, we twins were leaving home together, in the same car, sharing many items. The comfort of having each other as roommates helped us survive the dormitory and our freshman year. Different course schedules separated us and assisted in our independent growth, yet we still were secure in the knowledge that our twin brother was "home" with us at night, back at the dorm.

We twins continued sharing apartments during our sophomore and junior years at WVU. Even though we headed in opposite directions many times during undergrad school, sharing one vehicle never seemed to be a problem. As children, we each had duplicates of many items. However, more expensive items and objects, we shared together. It always seemed so effortless. From clothes early on, to high tech stereo equipment and then finally the car, we shared naturally and were respectful to one another. Always.

As you are already aware, during our third year of undergrad, Stanley was still majoring in Biology, hoping for a future in Optometry. Stephen was already in professional school, as a first year Pharmacy student. We lived in Pierpont apartments on the WVU Evansdale campus. Each day, Stephen would walk up to the Med Center, and Stanley would hitch-hike to the downtown campus. Yet we were still together; for evenings, weekends, dinner, rides home, and holidays. Even though our plans were different, we neither had ever really thought of "NOT" being together. When reality started to dawn on us, it was not palatable. In fact, to maintain the status quo, and just to keep his options open, Stanley applied and was accepted to Pharmacy school for the class behind Stephen. However, as you already know, Stanley decided to attend Optometry school in Chicago instead. We twins celebrated .... on the outside. The truth inside, remained unspoken. Our lives were about to change, forever!

Stanley takes it solo from here:

The car was completely packed and sitting in the driveway. Mom and Dad were ready to take me to Chicago. I was leaving. Stephen was staying. It was late August, 1979. WE were 21 years old. I become emotional; and tears flow as I type these words. I knew, down deep, in the essence that only we shared, that life would never be quite the same for us.

Until that moment, we were still intertwined, tight. It was first grade revisited in the driveway, only this time, we did what no supposed authority could ever do; we, with great difficulty, willfully separated!

I can see it and feel the moment as if it is occurring as I type. I was sitting in the back seat of the car, a Ford Escort, passenger side, with the door open, waiting for my parents. Having already bid farewell to Stephen during the packing process, I sat daydreaming, when suddenly, Stephen appeared, holding something in his hand. He crouched on the pavement adjacent to the car door. His face showed emotion. He hesitated, gathered himself, looked directly at me, furrowed his brow, then reached out his hand and clasped mine. He said, "Stanley, you be tough. Understand? You be tough." He released the held object and told me to take it and keep it close. It was a cross, made of wood from Jerusalem. Tears flowed down his cheeks as he then released my hand. As he rose to go back inside, he stressed, "You are my only brother, my twin brother. Be tough!"

I was crying as we pulled out of the driveway, clutching the wooden cross. On the way to Chicago, I pulled it on over my head and wore it as a necklace. I had heard what Stephen had just said, and I also knew what he had really meant. It was obvious to me because I understand "twin talk." He was worried about me, concerned about my well-being. He would miss me. He knew things were changing, …. forever. Stephen had told me that, …. he loved me, …. on that...*Separation Day*.

{Special note: The wooden cross is still in Stanley's possession. It is actually being borrowed by his son Chris and placed near his dorm room desk in college. It brings him comfort and peace when he is away from home as it did his Father 33 years earlier}

Let's Talk (We're Good at It)

Look up the word, "loquacious" in Webster's dictionary, and you will see a photograph of the Toompas Twins. We will take this opportunity to apologize to everyone who has suffered through some lengthy discussions through the years. Like one of our conversations, this chapter will "talk" about some unique aspects of our lives that have not been mentioned in any of the stories in either of our books. However, unlike our face-to-face meetings, you can actually "turn us off" by simply closing the book if you wish.

By the numbers, Mom and Stanley believe that "1" and "5" are significant. Stanley was the 1st twin born and 5 was always his favorite number as a child. As mentioned before, the metal house where we twins grew up was number 115. Then the house our parents moved to was 1105. Oddly enough, Stanley and Kim, when first married in 1981, moved to Chicago and lived at number 511. After moving back to West Virginia, Stanley moved to Philippi. Upon leaving our parent's house, he must travel on I-79 and then take exit

115! Stanley felt as though he was going "home." Through the years, when Stanley goes on trips, he will be randomly assigned floor 5 or room 15 a major percentage of the time. At dinners or banquets, he will wind up at table number 5 or 15. It seems an interesting coincidence.

In our first book we took a moment to reminisce about the many TV shows we enjoyed as kids. One we failed to mention was, "The Patty Duke Show."

Based on the premise of identical appearing cousins, we twins were absolutely sure that the show was based on us. We can still hear the theme song as we are writing this; *But they're cousins, identical cousins all the way, they laugh alike, they walk alike, at times they even talk alike, you can loose your mind, when cousins, are two of a kind!* Of course, we twins substituted the words "brother" for "cousins" and sang away!

Also, we twins were fans of the movie "The Parent Trap" whose identical twin story line captivated us.

Both Stanley and Stephen loved our World Book encyclopedias, or more specifically, any book that contained really cool, multiple, overlapping transparencies. Usually this involved the human body, one represented the vascular system, one the skeletal system, etc. Also, Dad, due to his status as a Pharmacist, was able to procure models of organs such as the heart, the eye, the kidney, as well as the knee joint and the hand. Many times we would retrieve these from our Dad's closet and "play" with them. The transparencies and the models both may have encouraged us to a future in a health care field. We do recall, that the models were borrowed by Mr. Kulczycki, for teaching purposes during 7th and 8th grade science class.

We remember Dr. Seuss books and have fond memories of trips to the Clarksburg Public Library with our Mom to check them out. When writing this manuscript, we were informed that Dr. Seuss had written a story about identical twins entitled, "Tadd and Todd." It is included in a book called "The Bippolo Seed and other lost stories" by Dr. Seuss.

Further down Pike Street from the library, sat the Robinson Grand and Ritz theaters. No mall cinemas or even the mall itself existed yet. We twins remember our Mom driving us to the theater as youngsters. Maybe "Herbie, The Love Bug" was featured. By the time we were in middle school we instructed Mom to drop us off in front of the library so we could walk the remaining distance to theater. Sometime she would acquiesce but if not, we would be ultimately embarrassed being let out of the car right in front of the theater. Looking back, it is difficult to remember why this action would embarrass us.

By the way, our first "real" dates occurred in 8th or 9th grade and involved Mom driving us to our girlfriends home, picking up our dates and then dropping us off at or near the theater. Holding hands with our dates in the dark theater dominates our memories more so than details of the "Planet of the Apes" sequels or the "Poseidon Adventure" movie we were watching. However, we did pay attention to Moe Howard, an original member of "The Three Stooges," and remember well his personal appearance at the Ritz Theater in 1973, less than 2 years before his death.

Dad consistently used Mobil gasoline, but we twins were always partial to the green Sinclair dinosaur logo vs. a blue flying winged Mobil horse!

The metal house we grew up in was detailed in our first book. However, one thing we failed to mention was the loud noise created if something hit the house. We twins would pass a football or Frisbee and if it would happen to hit the side of the house, the steel panel would reverberate and subsequently startle our Mother. She would then yell at us through the kitchen window, "Stop hitting the house! Can't you boys play croquet?"

As the years passed, one of us would stand in the backyard and one in the front and we threw a football over the house. Often our passes would be somewhat under-thrown and the football would hit the metal roof with quite a thud that would echo throughout the steel paneled house. Mom hated this unexpected, yet oft repeated, "sonic boom." Eventually the football gave way to us attempting to hit a wiffle ball over the house with a wooden bat, or throwing a baseball over the house. Mom seemed much more relaxed when we followed our Father's lead and began hitting small plastic golf balls with a pitching wedge or 9-iron over the house. When these light plastic balls hit the side or roof of the metal house, a much less objectionable sound was made.

We actually remember watching our Father practicing his golf swing and hitting real golf balls at a driving range that existed where Harry Green Chevy City is today on Bridgeport Hill. We twins enjoyed watching the modified/fortified jeep vehicle with a front plow driving around collecting the golf balls. We would urge Dad to try and hit the jeep!

As mentioned in our first book, we both married a girl named Kim, and we were married three months apart. Not mentioned however, is the fact that we served as each others best man. We have always assumed that all identical twins probably do this. In April of 1981, Stanley flew from Chicago via Pittsburgh to Bridgeport to attend Stephen's wedding. Always the more publically emotional one of the two, Stanley cried repeatedly at the reception when toasting his brother and his new bride. On the other hand, three months later in July, newlywed Stephen was much more composed when returning the favor during Stanley's wedding reception. Each Kim now had a twin, and the rest is history.

We twins have always thought that the traditional revolving doors to a hotel, such as The Stonewall Jackson Hotel in Clarksburg, were classy. By the way, the Sunday after church lunch buffet in the hotel basement was awesome, even for picky eaters like us.

There is no doubt, that when a Kentucky Fried Chicken restaurant finally came to Clarksburg, it was indeed just as advertised; "finger lick'n" good.

Also, we twins loved the revolving "bucket of chicken" sign!

In the bathroom at the metal house, on top of the cabinet in front of the mirror, was a small round shaped dish. On the rim was a representation of a black dachshund "wiener" dog that stretched all the way around the dish, until his snout almost touched his tail. This is one item from our youth that stands out to us.

Our cousin Leslie owned the coolest Jeep CJ and, believe it or not, let Stanley borrow it to use as a student council entry in the 1975 homecoming parade during our senior year in high school. In stark contrast to the Jeep, she also owned...you will not believe it...dying with anticipation aren't you...a vehicle of complete opposite aura...an American Motors...PACER! .... An American "CLASSIC."

In our first book, you learned that Bland's Drug Store delivered with a VW BUG. If this durable vehicle finally wore out, they replaced it with another. In contrast, Town and Country Drug Store used a rugged International Scout. The original one, corresponding with the store's opening, had a beautiful mural on each side of the back where the windows would have normally been. The mural depicted half town scene and half country scene with the words Town and Country overlaid respectfully. It was beautiful. Eventually, Datsun pick-ups, like the one Mr. Slinlor had, served as their delivery vehicles of choice.

Funny how life seems to always come full circle. Forty-five years later, Stanley's two children have vehicles; one is a Nissan (Datsun) pickup, the other a VW Bug!

The first air-conditioned car Dad owned was the white, 1965 ½ Dodge Custom 880. It was so hot in the metal house, that sometimes Dad would suggest that we hop in the car and take a drive, just to cool off. With not nearly as many cars on the road in the mid to late 60's, Dad enjoyed the drive as much as we did.

From 1960 onward, Dad drove Dodge cars. We twins loved going over to the Dodge garage to look at the new models in the showroom. Whether it be Chargers, Coronets, Polaras, Monacos, Challengers, Demons, or Darts, we loved all of the Dodge products as well as their neat emblems such as the "super bee." We also loved the Plymouth Dusters, Roadrunners, GTX's, and Barracudas. Our love of all things Mopar led us to be fans of drag racers, Sox and Martin. On one occasion, Dad took Stevie, Stanley, and some of the "Street Kids" to the local Eldora drag strip to see them drag their HEMI Cuda against "Grumpy" Jenkins' Camaro. Another of our favorite show vehicles was Bill Maverick's "Little Red Wagon." We had a model of this cool vehicle.

Speaking of cars, Uncle Bud always owned station wagons. We twins enjoyed riding on the tailgate of the green '58 Pontiac and the blue '67 Plymouth Fury.

The 60's was full of cool looking vehicles. We thought the coolest looking car was the 1965 Buick Riviera, because of the revolutionary hidden headlights at the time. Futuristic in appearance, we distinctly remember that the parents of our grade school classmate, Pam Baker, owned one. If her parents came early to pick her up from school, we would go to the window just to see the car's front grill in hopes that her Mom would turn on and/or off, the hidden headlights, so we could observe how they worked.

Speaking of the lights turned off, that reminded us of the time we were out driving our Dad's Dodge Monaco on I-79 with our buddies Eddie and Bernie. Up ahead we saw a familiar car driven by the Barnosky brothers, who were fraternal twins. We believe Eddie (undoubtedly) suggested to "blow their doors off." So, Stephen shoved the accelerator petal to the floor. The obvious and all to familiar sound of the four-barrel carburetor on the 383 kicked in and soon we were doing over 100 mph! We honked the horn as we blew by the other twins.

We had gone so far, so fast, that we had left them "in the dust." There was not a car in sight anywhere near us. Stephen slowed to legal speed and we all laughed and enjoyed our race victory for what seemed an eternity. But then, all of a sudden we hear a loud horn, and a car blows by us...with no headlights on! Fortunately, Stephen was not overly startled by this and maintained control of our car. As we approached the next exit, we saw they had pulled over, so we did likewise. Young and dumb, no seat-belts and in their case, no headlights. It is scary when we think back about it, but we did not give it a second thought at the time!

In our front yard at Mandan Road, stood a beautiful birch tree. We recall standing by the trees peeling off the multiple, white, ultra thin layers of bark. This was our Mom's favorite. It succumbed to a wide-spread birch blight, and on June 16, 1971, we chopped it down. Why do we know the exact date? Stanley saved two pieces of scrap, wrote the specifics on them and has kept them all these years! We guess we were not only attached to the metal house, but everything around it.

We both distinctly recall that when ill-behaved, our parent's would threaten that if the unacceptable pattern of behavior continued, we twins might end up in Pruntytown! As adults, we have discovered this may have been a common ploy utilized by most parent's in north-central West Virginia. Also, if we would ever champion a somewhat non-accepted notion, we would be chastened to quit thinking like that lest we end up in Weston! (We assume that most of our readers know that for decades, Pruntytown was a facility for wayward boys, and Weston was home to the state mental hospital.)

Actually, when Grandma Irene would baby sit, we would sometimes misbehave. This is, of course, after she had exhausted all attempts of entertainment like the aforementioned peeling of an apple in one continuous motion, or feeding Cindy the Chihuahua caffeinated coffee. Though upset, she would never threaten us with "Pruntytown" but would threaten telling our parents! Every time however, right before our parents were due to arrive home, she would assure us that if we would just be good for the next 15 minutes, she would not tell our parents .... and she never did! We verified this fact with our Mother. Grandma was honest!

Speaking of Grandma, she would get choked or start coughing, and as she began to straighten herself out, she sneezed. We thought this was hilarious and we laughed hysterically. Now, it happens to us at 53! She also worked as the resident director at DeSalles Hall in Clarksburg, which was the dorm for nursing students while training at St. Mary's Hospital. We twins loved running around and exploring that enormous building during those times when Mom would "hide" from storms there with Grandma.

We had a red metal swing set in our back yard growing up. Mom would watch us play from the kitchen window, while constantly yelling safety reminders. While playing, we might discover a turtle that had meandered into our back yard at Mandan Road. Placing him in a large tote box, which we "decorated" with crabgrass and clover, we would observe it for hours. We always hated to let it go. We found mother nature to be fascinating.

Picky eaters, we did love fresh sliced bologna from Betoni's Grocery on West Virginia Avenue.

In our first book, we wrote about the grade school era "Street Kids'. Upon entering junior high, we encountered new kids just around the block. We enjoyed hanging around Chuck Thomas, Gary Sokol, the Jackson brothers, John Benacossa, Rusty Rigsby, Don Byrd, Annette Flannigan, the Tuckers, Mark Mazzie, Michelle Shreves, Valinda Short, Cindy Rexroad, Mike Robey, Karen Louzy, Chuck Booth, Emily Berry, Alan McKinney, Crystal Pratt, Tammy Sullivan, Tim Booth, Wendy Losh, Danny Jenks, Mark Wolfe, Mark Spenser, Chuck Bray, Vanessa Scott, Roger Reeder, et al. Just what ever happened to Roger Reeder?

Though we do not have many fond memories of the Nutter Fort public pool, one positive recollection that puts a grin on our faces is Ole' Dear, otherwise known as Martha Davis. She always treated us kindly.

As children, we enjoyed visits by our cousin Lee Ann Gantner. She was a cheerful soul and delightful to be around. She would visit occasionally with Great Aunt Evelyn and we just loved her.

Our Mom always wanted us to take piano lessons. We totally rejected this idea. We told her that playing the piano was for sissies! Even so, we may have acquiesced if she would have offered to teach us herself, but she refused. Year later, ironically, our favorite musician became legendary pianist Elton John!

So, we grew up listening to contemporary pop music. We did not like Heavy Metal, really Hard Rock or Country. For example, we preferred "QUEEN" vs. "The KING." "STYX" but no "STONES." Bands with numbers in their names were favored over ones with colors. "THREE Dog Night" and "The FOUR Seasons" or "The FIFTH Dimension" instead of "BLUE Oyster Cult," "BLACK Sabbath" or "PINK Floyd, though "Deep PURPLE" was an exception to this rule. The "ELECTRIC Light Orchestra" jolted us more than "AC-DC." Cities were okay, such as "BOSTON," "CHICAGO," or "The ATLANTA Rhythm Section, but states such as "KANSAS" and "ALABAMA," not as much. "REO" and "CCR," beat "ELP" and "CSNY," and of course "RASPBERRIES" and "Bread" were more palatable than "Wild CHERRY." "The EAGLES" soared over "The BYRDS."

Truth be known, we related to "The CARPENTERS" more than we related to "The BOSS." JIM Croche beat JIMMY Buffett, and Tommy JAMES and the Shondells beat JAMES Taylor or The JAMES Gang. The better bad was "BAD Company" not "BADfinger," though we liked most bands beginning with the letter "B," such as "Beatles," "Beach Boys," "Bee-Gees," "Billy Joel," "Blood, Sweat and Tears," and "Bachman-Turner Overdrive." When it came to A's, "America" trumped "Aerosmith." Olivia Newton JOHN, and JOHN Denver were okay, but as we said, Elton JOHN was tops.

We enjoyed our "JOURNEY" on the "Grand Funk RAILROAD" more so than "CARS," or "Jefferson AIRPLANE", though "STARSHIP" was okay. Last but not least, we liked the "The GUESS WHO" vs. "The WHO," which always lead to discussions like this:

Friend: Do you like The Who?
Twins: No. The Guess Who.
Friend: Who?
Twins: No, Guess Who.
Friend: I did.
Twins: Who?
Friend: Doobie Brothers?
Twins: No, Guess Who.
Friend: Fleetwood Mac?
Twins: No, Guess Who.
Friend: I don't know, who?
Twins: No, The Guess Who.
Friend: I'm done. Guess who is crazy?
Twins: No, Guess Who isn't crazy, they are a good band.

Then the friend turns around and walks away.

It is appropriate that we make one final comment on the static-producing shocks at the old metal house that you are so very aware after reading both of our books. The spark produced really hurt! Stevie and Stanley would sometimes playfully shock one another but other times they would use this as a "weapon" of sorts. This could really lead to an argument. Also, friends loved the novelty of shocking us. Sometimes a spark created between your fingers and the wall was about one inch long and very visible. It reminded us of the famous "Lost in Space" Robot!

Through the years, many people have assumed that since we are identical twins, we probably possess an innate ability to more readily distinguish other sets of identical twins. Let us state for the record, that we are just as embarrassed and flummoxed, as people are with us, when encountering other sets of identical twins!

After reading two books full of Stevie - Stanley Stories, you may still have questions about our identical twin lives. Possibly, you may be an old classmate who would like to reconnect, or someone who might just like to make a comment, If so, we encourage you to get in contact with us and...*Let's Talk (We're Good at It)*

Twin Beds

The year is 2073. It is April Fool's Day. We twins are 115 years old today, and that is not an April Fool's joke! Sad to say, we have outlived our wives. Both Kims have gone to heaven already, finally relieved of their lifelong burdens of being married to identical twins. Even the children have passed on, all in their 80's. Of course, before we had our own individual families, we had each other, and that is just about all we have left now. The exception being, and fortunately so, that grandchildren do remain. In fact, Stanley's Grandson, Dean Christopher Toompas, who was born in the year 2020 (appropriate for an Optometrist's grandson!) is now 53 and is visiting us on our birthday. Sad over the passing of his own Father, Chris, and responsible for both of us, he decided to place Grandpa Stanley and Great Uncle Stevie into a nursing home a few months ago .... together!

While conversing, Dean remembers that we twins wrote a couple books many years ago and asks what they were called. Great Uncle Stevie responds, "I'm The One The Other Isn't, The Stevie - Stanley Stories." Grandpa Stanley adds, "Yes Dean, and we were your age when we wrote them!" Dean says he remembers his Father reading bedtime stories to him from the first book when he was really young, and that he read the second book himself when he was in middle school. He had not seen one for years but that he would check with his Mom and see if any remained in his Dad's library.

Speaking of reading, we twins both see decently well with old glasses that Stanley had made before he retired. Though on just a few prescription medications, they are all delivered from Town and Country Drug Store, long since sold by Stephen.

Having brought a birthday cake made by his wife, Dean cuts it and gives a piece to both Stanley and Stephen. Of course, Stanley demands the first piece, since he WAS born first. It is a chocolate cake with the 7-minute, homemade, white, vanilla icing from our Mom's original recipe, handed down through the generations.

While enjoying the cake, Stephen notices that an antique auto auction is being televised on TV. He turns up the volume to a level somewhat uncomfortable for Dean, and we begin watching the show together. Some beautiful American cars are being auctioned that day, including many we twins remember from our childhood including a Mercury Cougar, Chevy Camaro, and Pontiac GTO, all with hidden headlights. Then we see a Plymouth Barracuda, Dodge Charger, and then a very rare Ford Pinto appears. We twins about choke on our birthday cake! Dean is confused concerning our sudden state of euphoria. Stephen explains that a 1974 Ford Pinto was OUR first car. Just like the birthday cake, white on the outside and black on the inside, the "White Goddess" as we called it, certainly invokes wonderful memories from our youth.

Bored, Dean grabs the remote and changes the channel to the pre-game, Final Four coverage. That's just fine with us, though we were disappointed that West Virginia had gotten beat in the Regionals. Maybe next year WVU's basketball team can finally win that elusive second nation title to go along with the 2044 National Championship won by the Mountaineers.

We mute the volume, finish our cake and then Dean asks both of us if we mind sharing the small room together. We both laugh and remind him that we had shared a much smaller room in the metal house while growing up. Back then we shared a trundle bed and frequently one of us fell down onto the other through the night. At least here, in the nursing home, we both have our own beds, all the time, by ourselves! Anyway, we were both born small and skinny, and have remained small and skinny our entire life, so there is plenty of space. We do become "chilled" quite easily due to our frailness. If so, we just pull on a cardigan sweater and instantly think the exact same thought... "DAD!"

Of course, we have not shared a room together in over 90 years, so it has taken a little adjustment. The worst part about living together in an extended care facility, is that none of the nurses nor any of the staff can tell us apart, so they put name-tags on everything. Similar to our birth, they also designate Stanley's bed as "A" and Stephen's bed as "B."

One day, Stephen decided that we should change beds to fool them, like we did to our teachers back in Nutter Fort Grade School. Well, the staff never noticed, so after a few hours, we just changed back. Our Physician is more observant, as he is aware of the very, very faint "1 inch" scar on Stephen's forehead, the result of an unfortunate ironing board accident 112 years ago.

Even though we twins both have high cholesterol, which Stephen took medication for through the years but Stanley always refused, amazingly neither of us have had any major health problems. Also, neither of us has fallen in the nursing home. Considering just how uncoordinated we were as children, this too seems amazing. The Doctor attributes this rare feat of living to be 115 years old, to our aging processes being uniquely affected by some sort of electro-magnetic phenomena induced by the metal house we were raised in for the first two decades of life. Of course, we give all the credit for our longevity to our outstanding parents and wonderful families that we were both blessed with. God certainly had a nice plan for our lives.

We twins have pictures and photos hanging on the walls and we inform Dean that while growing up we had nothing on the drab, gray enameled-coated steel bedroom walls of our metal house for most of our childhood. Just about the time we were in junior high school, our Mom purchased some small little red magnets in the shape of ladybugs. The magnets were weak, but they did hold individual sheets of paper. So we put homemade signs on our walls and pages from sports magazines. Dean says that he remembers "magazines" from his childhood and that he actually saved a few. Valuable now, very collectable, as the print media in America has long since vanished.

We tell Dean that 5 days ago, a new janitor came in to clean the restroom. Stephen was in there at the time, so he stands, waiting in front of the empty bed. He then looks over at Stanley and says, "So, old twin, which one are you?" Stanley, knowing he is too feeble to run, yet obstinate at this advanced age, replies, "I'm the one the other isn't!" The janitor appears bemused, shakes his fist at Stanley, turns and walks out.

Dean notices that neither of us talk as much (thank goodness) as we did when we served our respective communities as health care professionals, yet always seem to understand what the other twin is feeling, wanting or thinking. A sort of private communication. Kind of ODD, yet we can not EVEN begin to explain it to him. By the way, every time a severe thunder & lightning storm occurs, we just turn to each other, smile, and then simultaneously speak the same one word... "MOM!"

Before leaving, Dean gives both of we frail, approximately 104 lbs twins (just as at birth, Stephen weighs 5 oz. more than Stanley) a careful, measured hug. As he does so, he says that he misses his Father Chris, but can not really discern which one of us that Chris most resembled? We both tell him that we love him as he leaves the room.

Wearing identically patterned flannel pajamas, albeit, Stephen's green and Stanley's blue, with a smile on our faces and some 7-minute, homemade, white, vanilla icing also, we twins fall asleep.

That night, their birthday becomes their death day, as both Stanley and Stephen pass away. Stanley dies first, then Stephen, twenty minutes later, while sound asleep, eternally inseparable, in their...*Twin Beds*.

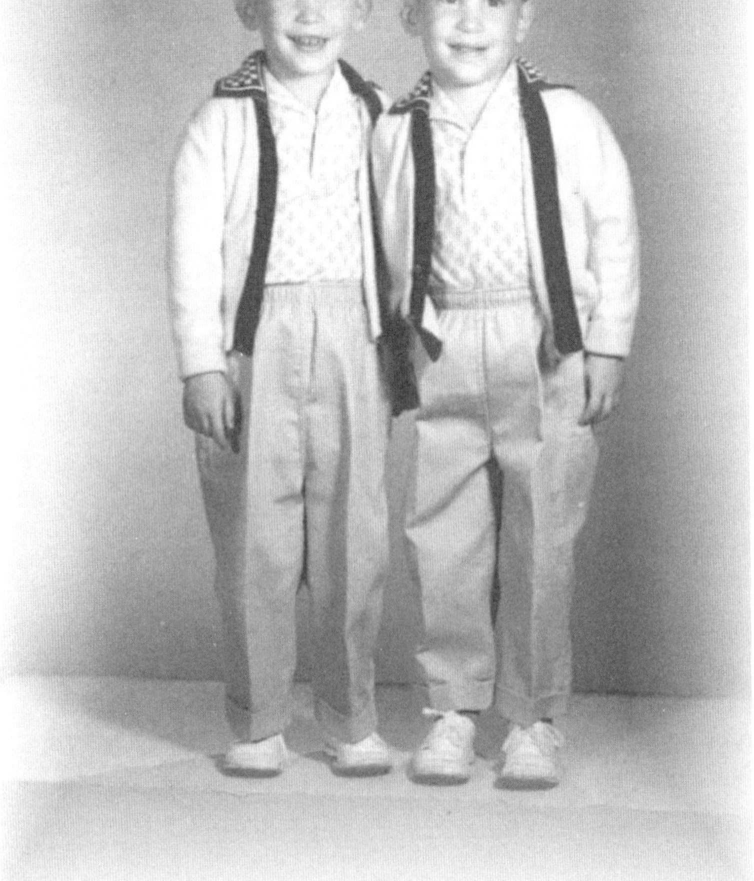

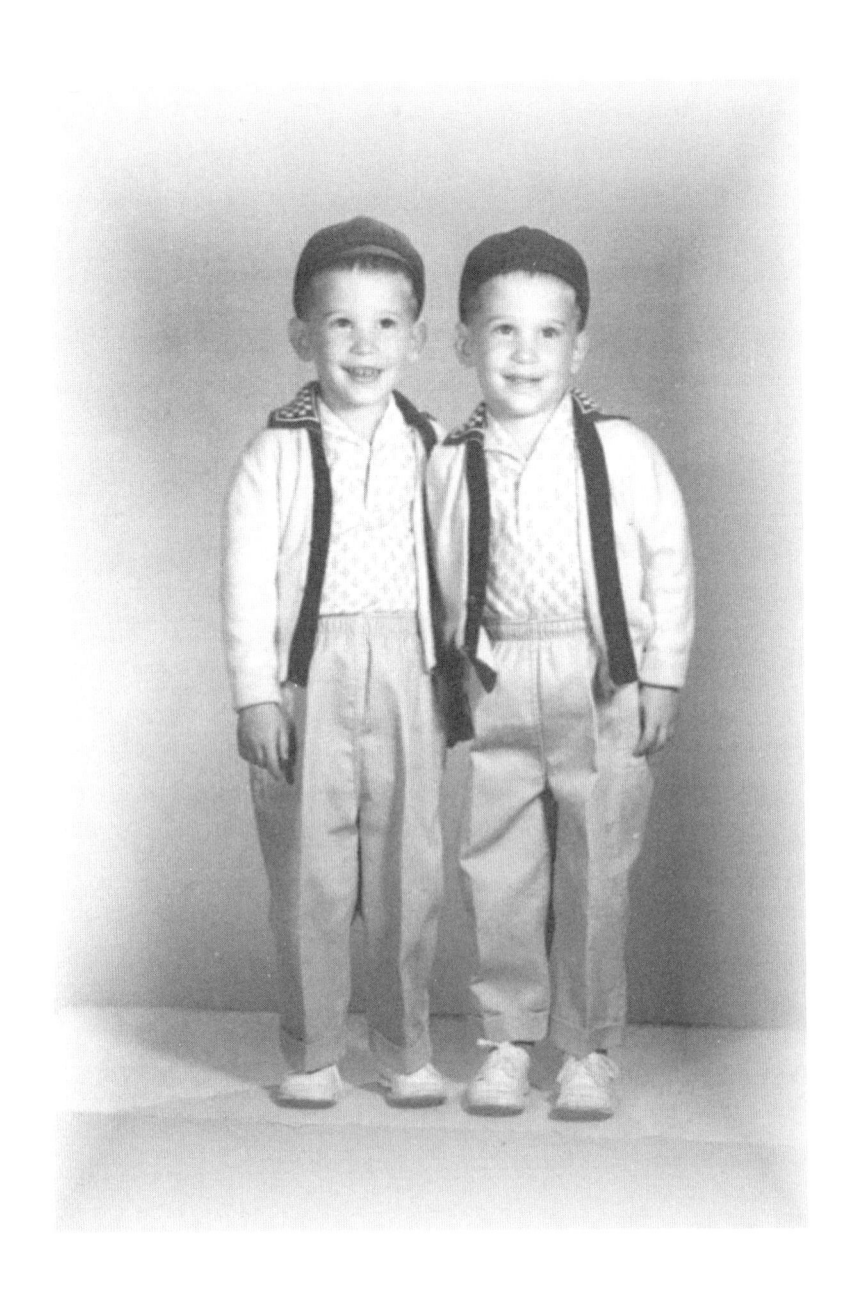